The Reflective Disciple

The Reflective Disciple

*Learning to live as faithful followers of Jesus
in the twenty-first century*

Roger L. Walton

 EPWORTH

Scripture quotations are from the New Revised Standard Version of
the Bible, copyright 1989 by the Division of Christian Education of
the National Council of the Churches of Christ in the USA. Used by
permission. All rights reserved.

British Library Cataloguing in Publication data

A catalogue record for this book is available
from the British Library

978 0 7162 0648 4

First published in 2009
by Epworth Press
Methodist Church House
25 Marylebone Road
London NW1 5JR

Typeset by Regent Typesetting, London
Printed and bound in Great Britain by
CPI Antony Rowe, Chippenham, SN14 6LH

Contents

Acknowledgements   ix

Introduction   xi

1   The Dialogue of Discipleship   1

2   The Context of Our Discipleship   28

3   A Fresh Picture of God   51

4   The Rhythm of Discipleship   82

5   The Reflective Disciple   111

6   Christian Communities in which Disciples Grow   143

v

Dedicated to Bill Denning (1934–2007)
who taught me much about being a
reflective disciple

Acknowledgements

Many people have helped this book to appear. It would be foolish to try to name all of them, for some have contributed by small conversations, others by gentle encouragement and kindly patience, some have inspired by the practice of their Christian discipleship and others have read drafts and debated ideas with me. Almost certainly in an attempt to name all I would miss a vital contributor. I want simply to make mention of a few. My colleagues at the Wesley Study Centre, Jocelyn Bryan and Andrew Lunn, helped me make time to work on this text by shouldering work that would have fallen to me, and students of Cranmer Hall and the Wesley Study Centre who read early drafts of chapters and offered their enthusiastic and honest comments. Jeff Astley and James Dunn set me off on the project, while Julie Lunn and Adrian Smith spent many hours reading the chapters of the book and helping me express my ideas more clearly. My wife, Marion and my adult children, Laura and Andrew, also believed in the enterprise and shared in the proofreading. I am grateful to all these and a host more people. Any persisting faults are however entirely my own doing.

Introduction

Splendid are those who take sides with the poor:
They are citizens of the Bright New World.
Splendid are those who grieve deeply over misfortunes:
The more deeply they grieve, the stronger they become.
Splendid are the gentle:
The world is safe in their hands.
Splendid are those who have a passion for justice:
They will get things done.
Splendid are those who make allowances for others:
Allowances will be made for them.
Splendid are those who seek the best for others and not themselves:
They will have God for company.
Splendid are those who help enemies to be friends:
They will be recognized as God's true children.
Splendid are those who have a rough time of it because they stand up
for what is right:
They too are citizens of the Bright New World.

Matthew 5.3–12, *Good as New* translation[1]

On 16 October 2007 *The Guardian* G2 magazine carried a
story about the England rugby team. This was not surprising,
as it was the week before the final of the World Cup in which
England were to play South Africa. There was a bit of rugby
fever all that week, made more intense by the fact that England had performed dismally in the opening stages of the
competition and then gone on, against all the odds, to beat
both Australia, the favourites, and France, the hosts. In the
lead up to the match, the article was exploring how well the
teams represented the countries whose names they carried, in
terms of the range of people in the squads. Attempting to show
how inclusive and representative the England team was, there

---

1 John Henson, *Good as New*, Washington/Winchester: O Books,
2004, p. 129.

were short profiles of players, including one on Jason Robinson who, according to the journalist, was 'proof that the squad can absorb a player from any background'. Robinson was presented as 'different' in two ways. First, he was a working-class lad from Chapeltown, Leeds, born of a white mother and black father he never knew and, second, he had become a 'born-again Christian who now eschews nights out with his team mates in favour of a takeaway pizza and Bible study in his room'.[2]

There are several things of interest in this journalistic snippet. First, there is an assumption that to be a Christian is somehow different and odd. A century earlier it would have been almost unthinkable to suggest that being a Christian and playing rugby for England were somehow strange or incompatible attributes. Now, it seems, people professing Christian faith are perceived as unusual and it is an exceptional case when such people can be included in a national team. Ironically, attitudes to faith may have moved in the opposite direction to the other 'difference' noted about Jason Robinson: his ethnic and working class origins. It is not difficult to believe that the racist attitudes prevalent in the structure of our society would have made it very difficult for someone who was born of a white mother and black father to reach the top of the sporting world in Britain even 40 years ago despite his or her outstanding talent. One hopes that this may have changed profoundly, though the article may bear witness to a continued prejudice. If, on the other hand, the journalist intended to say that now talent wins out, then it makes the view on faith even more striking. For, while attitudes that discriminated and excluded on the basis of ethnic or class background may be being broken, during the same period, being a Christian has increasingly been seen as odd and marginal. British Society has changed profoundly in its view of religion. The media now regularly portrays Christian faith as quaint – a curious hangover from the past; or quirky – the unusual interest of a few; or even dangerous – a view of life that only brings division or destruction or holds human-

---

2 Richard Williams, 'True Colours', *The Guardian* G2, 16 October 2007, pp. 4–6.

ity up in its progress.[3] It should be clear that to choose to be a follower of Jesus today will not be done to court popularity and gain society's approval. To be a disciple today in the UK is often to be at odds with the wider culture, and thus the path is a hard one to take.

Second, the article's cameo of what it means to be a Christian is interesting. According to this brief picture of Jason Robinson, following Jesus is not about drinking or having a good night out with the lads but is about studying the Bible. Even if the report is inaccurate about Jason's Christian lifestyle, these phrases in the article suggest that being Christian, in most people's minds, takes a concrete and discernible form. There are things you do and things you do not do, which mark out that you are a follower of Christ. In other words, discipleship is to do with identifiable practices – regular activities, actions and attitudes – that characterize the life of a Christian.

Most Christians would want to add to this brief and perhaps misleading set of characteristics. Many would include the practice of forgiveness, loving one's neighbour and witnessing to faith. Others would stress the struggle for justice for all people, especially the poor and vulnerable. Some might include the practices of fasting, or regular sharing in the Eucharist, or embracing non-violence as a way of life. There would be many that would point to the beatitudes (good attitudes and actions) quoted at the beginning of this introduction. Perhaps all would want to cite the practice of prayer and worship as a feature of Christian life. Jeff Astley[4] identifies a range of attributes that includes beliefs, actions, attitudes and emotions which together constitute what it means to be Christian. Thus, Christians, as well as those who observe them, accept that discipleship is, at least in part, located in a set of characteristics and practices.

---

3 See for example Richard Dawkins, *The God Delusion*, Maidenhead: Black Swan, 2007. Christopher Hitchens, *God is Not Great*, London: Atlantic Books, 2007. Sam Harris, *The End of Faith*, London: The Free Press, 2005.

4 Jeff Astley, *The Philosophy of Christian Religious Education*, London: SPCK, 1994.

There are some intriguing features missing from this mini-ature sketch of Christian discipleship. Notice that it speaks of Jason Robinson becoming a Christian but tells us nothing about the story of this change. How did it happen, who was involved, what experience did he go through and how did this change his relationship to God? All this is hidden from us, and while the author cannot be indicted for not telling us everything about Jason Robinson's faith story – he was after all writing about rugby – the one-line summary of Christian commitment he offers us omits some vital ingredients.

One can find out a little more about Jason Robinson's conversion. Apparently, another great rugby player had a con-siderable influence on him. Va'aiga Tuigamala, nicknamed Inga the Winger, was a team mate of Jason Robinson at Wigan and his quiet contentment with life made a big impression on Robinson.[5] It was not until later that Robinson became a Christian himself but the relationship and what he saw in his team mate was important. Through this he sensed and discov-ered a relationship with God for himself. I can say that for myself there was a similar journey. I met a group of Christians and while one could identify some practices and activities that marked them out, it was not the outward attributes or even the inner attitudes that were the most attractive – some were singularly unappealing, as they looked like hard work – but I was attracted by the sense that the Christian people I had met had a living relationship with Christ that enlivened them and steered them through life. This was the vital factor in my becoming a Christian and discovering the reality of that living relationship with God for myself. This adds a third piece to the jigsaw of discipleship today. Discipleship is always a human story, a life journey that finds its meaning and is animated by the relationship at its heart.

The other bit we can't see from the vignette is what kind of God it is that Jason Robinson believes in. It is clearly the Chris-tian God, the one who is known through Jesus, but what is this God like, what is God's essential character, how does God act

---

5 Bob Howitt, *Inga the Winger*, Auckland: Rugby Press, 1993.

in the world and what does trusting in this God imply for our lives? If we want to understand and practise Christian discipleship, the picture of God at the centre of that way of life is of crucial importance. Only by knowing something of the God revealed in Jesus can disciples live by trust in God.

These four elements, which this newspaper article helped highlight, are all aspects of interwoven threads in discipleship:

- Discipleship is always lived in a particular context, place and time.
- Discipleship is manifest through practices (attitudes and actions) in everyday life.
- Discipleship is living out faith in a real human story.
- Discipleship is deeply related to the view of God at its centre.

Of course, these are not separate and discrete features. They are closely intertwined and each affects the others. For example, how you view God will be shaped by the faith practices that you engage in and by the cultural context in which you live. On the other hand, the picture of the God you trust may alter how you practise faith and influence what within the culture you embrace and what you resist. In a particular life story all the other three elements will constantly be shaping or being filtered by the particular demands and opportunities of the person's life. There is a dynamic relationship between the strands, always moving and changing.

My desire in writing is to offer a portrayal of Christian discipleship for today and to do this it is necessary to scrutinize these four elements and so to separate them out to a degree, in order to do some detailed work on their realities. In the book I have chosen to explore these four threads in a slightly different order from the one listed above. Chapter 2 addresses context; Chapter 3 explores our picture of God; while Chapter 4 looks at faith lived in human life stories and leads to a discussion of practices. Chapter 5 continues to discuss Christian practices with an exploration of what it is to be a reflective disciple and what it means to practise faithful reflection. Chapters 1 and 6 stand outside this linear sequence. Chapter 1 is an examination of discipleship in the New Testament and Chapter 6 is a vision of a Church for the nurture of disciples. The first argues that the New Testament bears witness to the dialogical nature of discipleship and suggests a model that underpins the approach to Chapters 2–5. Chapter 6 draws out the implications of the argument of the book for the Church. You may choose to read these in the order they appear or come back to them having explored the central chapters. Much will depend on how you like to approach ideas. If the Bible is always your starting point, begin with Chapter 1, if experience is your normal launching pad, start with Chapter 2. Naturally, at some point these should meet but you can choose when and how.

Précis of the book: to help navigate and choose your route

Chapter 1, 'The Dialogue of Discipleship', is a study of discipleship in the New Testament. The chapter poses and explores three different questions: (1) What was the original call to discipleship about? (2) Was discipleship always the same in every Christian Community? (3) How was discipleship worked out in new places and times? The first question leads us to some insights about the calling to be disciples and the kingdom of God. The second gets into the interesting area of how New Testament writers portray discipleship to be different in different contexts. The third question explores some of the dynamics of learning discipleship. I conclude three things from this study:

1 It is difficult to state what form discipleship takes in all circumstances. There are recurring features, which provide benchmarks or reference points, but discipleship must be worked out in particular situations.
2 There is a relationship between what we say about God and how we practise discipleship. That is, our vision of God inspires and orients our discipleship.

3 Christian discipleship is to be discovered in the midst of a living dialogue as we look to Jesus and the traditions we have inherited on the one hand and our context on the other.

These points are then explored for our own time and place in Chapters 2–6.

Chapter 2, 'The Context of Discipleship', addresses the **context** of Britain in the early twenty-first century. The deep wariness that contemporary culture holds for Christian faith has to be acknowledged and understood. If it is not, it will continue to erode confidence and undermine individuals and churches. Many of the dilemmas that people of faith face are a direct result of the changes that have come about in Britain in the last 100 years. The chapter begins by telling the stories of six disoriented disciples, highlighting some of the tensions in their Christian faith as it encounters everyday life. I then stand back from the individual experiences and attempt to describe some of the overarching changes and challenges of our own age. Under the three headings of post-national, post-modern and post-Christendom, I describe the changes our culture has undergone in the last 50 years and draw out some of the implications and challenges for disciples. The key argument here is that disciples are faced with an unfamiliar and rapidly changing reality in which it is not easy to see how best to live out discipleship. We who are seeking to follow Jesus are on the forefront of rediscovering the essence and daily practice of Christian faith. This means that there are no easy, pat answers, no pre-formulated words that will resolve our dilemmas for us. Rather, the calling of discipleship is to engage with our daily problems and challenges and bring them into a conversation with our faith tradition to find fresh ways of living out faith. We do not retreat from difficult quandaries but meet them with confidence that the God we trust is at work already and that there is a faithful way of responding to the challenge.

Chapter 3, 'A Fresh Picture of God', seeks to refresh **our picture of God** by looking at the notions of the missionary God (*missio Dei*) and God the Trinity. I argue that God who is known in Jesus is active in the life of the world as well as the Church. This triune God invites us to join in this outward moving mission and discover our true selves by participating in God's transformative action. This renewed vision of God is already giving new ideas and directions to the Church but we need to maintain a robust view of the *missio Dei* as speaking to us through the world as well as through the Church's revelation, if we are to avoid an insular or imperialist stance. The second half of the chapter offers ways of holding on to the notion of the missionary God who meets us in the midst of everyday life.

The challenge of living out **faith in a real human story** is our concern in Chapter 4, 'The Rhythm of Discipleship'. The chapter opens by drawing attention to the fragmented nature of reality that most of us know in ordinary living – in home, family, work and church. We often experience ourselves as different people in different settings and spheres of life. Two common ways of responding to this post-modern sense of the divided self – compartmentalism and fundamentalism – are rejected and then I sketch out a view of discipleship as most meaningful when located in a rhythm of a gathering and dispersing people of God. We are gathered and then sent into the world to seek and proclaim God's presence, to form and be formed in the likeness of Christ, to translate the languages of the world and the faith and to be the travellers and traders learning and helping others to learn of the reality of God. The final section of Chapter 4 sets out **the practices** that disciples need to develop to sustain their calling: courageous openness, careful accountability, conscientious immersion in the tradition and constant prayerfulness.

Chapter 5, 'The Reflective Disciple', continues the exploration **practices** through focusing on the role of 'faithful reflection' in discipleship. By exploring the nature of reflection in human life and then illustrating how this works in people's faith experience I draw out six key aspects of faithful reflection and suggest ways to nurture reflective habits in our discipleship. This chapter holds up the image of the reflective disciple as a model for living a faithful Christian life.

The final chapter, 'Christian Communities in which Disciples Grow', asks what kind of church communities form reflective disciples called to transform and be transformed in the world? Here three different callings of the Church are examined: (1) the call to be a kingdom community (2) the call to be a missionary body and (3) the call to nurture and equip disciples. There is a key role here for Christian education, but Christian education in a much broader way than it is often defined. Each equally important calling of the Church is considered and suggestions made about the kinds of Christian education that will cultivate and cherish this calling.

Who is this book for?

This book is not primarily aimed at inviting people to embrace Christian faith for the first time, though if that were the outcome for you, I would be delighted. Rather, it is written for those who have already taken the first steps in following Jesus and for some who have been on the road a long time, who need to pause and reflect on what it is they are doing and how to perceive and continue the journey they are already on. My sincere hope is that it will help you consider discipleship anew and encourage you to travel as a reflective disciple.

I began this introduction by quoting the beatitudes from Matthew 5 in the *Good as New* translation by John Henson. The first time I heard this read aloud it made my spine tingle. I was already very familiar with the beatitudes. I had studied them in English and Greek and with the help of various commentaries. I had preached on them and reflected on them many times in relationship to my own discipleship. They contain an implicit call to follow Jesus and to practise Christian faith in the midst of the pain and unfinished nature of the world. John Henson's translation made me hear that call again in fresh, urgent tones and in a way that spoke immediately to the micro and macro worlds in which I live. The translation is an icon of 'faithful reflection'. Here a committed follower of Jesus seeks to speak and act faithfully out of a conversation between the faith tradition and the contemporary context. To live and act in ways that make clear and fresh the way of Jesus today is the mark of a reflective disciple.

The Dialogue of Discipleship

There is a story told of a man taking his young son for a walk. The child was curious about everything around him and asked lots of questions. As they passed a building site the son noticed a high crane controlled by a man in a cockpit hundreds of feet above the ground. He asked his father, 'How does the man get up into the crane, Dad?' His father looked up and said to his son, 'I don't know how he gets up there.' They walked on and the young boy's interest was captured by a huge sculpture in the town square. It was of a woman riding on a horse and carrying a flag. The boy wanted to know 'Who is she?' 'Why is she carrying a flag?' 'When was this statue made?' 'I'm sorry to say that I don't know', said the man to each of the questions. Now they were in the park and great oaks towered over. 'What makes trees grow so high, Dad?' was the question posed by the boy. 'I'm afraid I don't know', said the father. The child became quiet for a time, though they walked on together happy in each other's company. Eventually the boy said, 'Do you mind me asking all these questions, Dad? 'No, certainly not,' said his father, warmly, 'if you don't ask questions, you never learn anything.'

The amusing irony in the story is, of course, that asking the questions in this particular case did not bring much learning. Or did it? Perhaps the child was learning that grown ups don't know the answers to all questions. Maybe he was discovering that there were some questions that your dad can't answer but others perhaps could. He might discover later (or have already realized) that there are other questions that only your mum or dad can answer. It is possible that on this walk of discovery he was beginning to learn about questions: what kind of questions to ask of whom and how to form the right questions to ask of the appropriate source. Most important, he was encouraged by a person he loved and trusted to carry on with his inquiring to find the knowledge that he wanted or needed.

We begin our study of discipleship by taking some questions to the Bible, and in particular the New Testament. Our intuition tells us that there must be much to learn about discipleship here, for in its pages we encounter Jesus who calls, and we meet the first disciples to respond to his call. Here also we have a record of the words of Paul and other early church leaders to some of the earliest converts on how to live as Christians. In these writings, too, we become aware of the problems that these early disciples faced and over which they sometimes stumbled.

The issue is what questions to ask.

The central question of this book is: How should we live as disciples of Jesus today? This is not an easy question to put to the New Testament in a direct way, however, for the assumption in our question is that the answer will speak immediately to the particularities of our modern age, some of which, as we shall see in Chapter 2, were unknown to these early Christian writers. If put by the young boy in our story, it is a question that might evoke the response, 'I don't know.' This does not mean that there is nothing to learn about discipleship in the New Testament – far from it. Rather, it may mean that we have to refine our question to elicit what it is that the New Testament can tell us. In order to do this, let us for a moment consider the nature of the New Testament.

What questions can the New Testament answer?

The New Testament is made up of accounts of the life and ministry of Jesus written 30–60 years after his death, together with a series of letters sent by Paul and other Christian leaders between AD 30 and 100, and an apocalyptic vision, which we call Revelation. These writings were circulated in the early Church and used in worship and teaching and finally fixed into an authorized or canonical collection in the third century. In other words, some of these writings were written close to the life and death of Jesus and probably drew on oral and written records that were closer still. Others were written to Christian communities a long time after the first apostles were dead in order to pass on the good news and help Christians live out their calling to follow Christ in their particular time and place.

Described thus, there are some questions we may be able to put to the New Testament that may help us in our endeavour:

1 What was the original call to discipleship about?
2 Was discipleship always the same in every Christian community?
3 How was discipleship worked out in new places and times?

Let us look at each question in turn and see where they lead us.

Q1: What was the original call to discipleship about?

When Jesus called those first disciples by the Sea of Galilee what was he calling them to be and do? In his book *Jesus' Call to Discipleship* James Dunn[1] has set out a picture of what we can know about the call to the first disciples. He describes this call under three broad themes.

A call to recognize the reality of God's kingdom

First, Jesus' call was to recognize the reality of God's kingdom. This was central to Jesus' preaching and ministry (Mark 1.14–15). As a translation 'kingdom' may be too static and territorial. The original Aramaic contains this idea but is much broader and we might be better to speak of the rule or reign of God. However it is translated, the centrality of the notion to Jesus' preaching and teaching is widely agreed. The rule of

---

1 James D. G. Dunn, *Jesus' Call to Discipleship*, Cambridge and New York: Cambridge University Press, 1992.

God, the patterning of God's justice, peace and truth was, said Jesus, at hand, imminent, and calling for an urgent response. The right response was to repent and believe. Repentance means more than a change of mind and regret for things done wrong. It involves 'turning around' and heading in a new direction, a complete life change, unconditional and comprehensive. The invitation that Jesus gave was to discern the reality of God's rule breaking in and to live a new life in its light.

This was the general message of Jesus in which the specific calls of individual disciples are to be understood. Andrew, Peter, James and John and the others are called to be with Jesus to learn of the in-breaking way of God, to be his assistants in proclaiming and serving the kingdom of God. Jesus himself was the prophet and proclaimer, focus and agent of this rule of God and to be a disciple, to follow Jesus, was to share Jesus' calling and destiny, to join him in proclaiming the kingdom and in confronting the people with the kingdom's good news and imminent judgement.[2]

A call to be alongside the poor and sinners

Second, says Dunn, the kingdom was announced to two groups in particular: the poor and sinners. The poor according to the Hebrew scriptures comprised the materially impoverished, the economically and politically powerless and those who recognized their own weakness and looked to God. In these writings there were also responsibilities and principles laid out for God's people to uphold: namely to provide for the poor, to condemn the oppression of the poor and to affirm God as the champion of the poor. Jesus upheld these ideas but went further in seeing the kingdom as being proclaimed to the poor now (Luke 4), and in pronouncing the poor as blessed by God, who is giving them the kingdom (Luke 6.20 cf. Matthew 5.3). The authenticity of Jesus' own messianic claim was precisely that the poor have good news preached to them (Matthew 13). Disciples

---

2 Martin Hengel, *The Charismatic Leader and His Followers*, New York: Crossroad, 1981, pp. 72–4.

were thus called to be with Jesus alongside the poor, giving to the poor, protecting the dignity of the poor and celebrating with the poor the signs of the kingdom among them. They were to live by different values in the world, where material possessions might be a distraction from the task. Those who do nothing to help the poor were condemned by Jesus and, at the same time, Jesus offered an opportunity to live life in a new power where 'we cease finding our life in what we own and control, and begin to live out of God's wealth of spirit and for God's kingdom'.[3]

As well as the poor, disciples were to join Jesus in welcoming sinners. Sinners in the New Testament are best understood as those who broke or disregarded the law. This was not simply a matter of breaking the law as a set of rules but, as the law was an expression of the covenantal relationship between God and the people of Israel, violation of the law was disrespecting the covenant. Living the law was a sign of belonging to God's people, breaking the law was disregarding the covenant. Clearly, therefore, Gentiles were sinners in the sense that they were outside the covenant relationship. Jews too could be sinners, if they broke the law. The problem of Jesus' day was that the defining of the boundaries of the people of God had become more restricted, narrow and exclusive. Jesus took a stand in opposition to these narrowly defined views of the law and this gave rise to some of his fiercest opposition (Mark 2.23—3.6). He was a friend of tax collectors and sinners, he ate meals with them and let an 'unclean' woman wash his feet. He talked with women and put a child in the midst of the disciples as a model of discipleship. Jesus welcomed and included those who had been put outside either by others' rules or by themselves. He taught that forgiveness is to be given over and over again and said that in the kingdom of God the one who serves is greatest, pointing to himself as the chief example (Mark 10.35–45). Disciples who shared Jesus' proclamation of the kingdom were to be like Jesus in welcoming and including those marginalized

---

3 Dunn, *Jesus' Call to Discipleship*, p. 54.

by society, to let love be the touchstone of living the law, to forgive, to serve and to be open to and respecting of all.

A call to participate in God's kingdom community

The third theme in Dunn's account is about corporate life. There is for the disciples a way of living together that in itself points to the kingdom. For example, there was no hierarchy within the community save that Jesus was the leader and focus. Disciples are not in any sense in an intermediary position. People all had direct access to Jesus and attempts to prevent them coming are rebuked. Moreover, there was no real distinction between those who literally followed him and a much wider circle of disciples. Anyone who does the will of God belongs to the community (Mark 3.32–5). Thus, the community must not see itself as exclusive but open to outsiders, 'beyond the more obvious and more formal identity markers'.[4] Another feature of community life was its essentially missionary orientation. They had a job to do. The twelve were sent out to preach. Others stayed at home to pray and to provide hospitality for the mission. The wider community of followers is a community supporting those active in evangelism and being active missionaries themselves in the quality of lives they lead – salt, light etc. (Matthew 5.13–16). Finally, the Jesus community is marked by suffering. The way of Jesus was to the cross and the followers of Jesus were also to take up the cross, deny themselves and follow him.

An answered question?

Here then is a reconstructed picture of what discipleship meant for the very first disciples. Jesus called them to recognize the reality of God's rule in the world around them, to repent and to believe, to share in the proclamation of the kingdom and to learn to live out the truth in action. Close to the poor and bridging the boundaries to those on the edge, the disciples were

---

4 Dunn, *Jesus' Call to Discipleship*, p. 111.

to be with and act like Jesus. They were called to exercise forgiveness and practise costly humble service, to live with each
other in a way that was non-hierarchical and open, to be fully
committed to the Jesus mission, even ready to face suffering.

We have an answer to our question. We can sketch what
being called to follow Jesus meant for those first disciples who
heard and followed him. This is useful to us, for it provides us
with some reference points for our discipleship – the kingdom
or rule of God, closeness to the poor, openness to sinners, and
participation in a community that lives by a set of alternative
values. These elements in turn help to anchor our discipleship
with the first Christians. But as soon as we try to put these
features into our setting, some questions come to the fore.
For example, what does it mean to proclaim God's kingdom
today? Who are the poor in the twenty-first century and how
can we declare the kingdom to the poor? What does 'sinners'
mean now – it cannot mean exactly what it meant then because
the notion of a sinner had a particular meaning in that society
and its history. Should we take it to mean someone who com-
mits any kind of sin or would it be better to think about those
who are marginalized now? If we think its primary meaning is
related to the marginalized, does it refer to any marginalized
person or only to those marginalized through religion? What
form does the kingdom community take now and does it map
to the Church? All these are question of translation, which
need to be addressed because there is large time gulf between
Jesus' first call and today. As Dunn himself writes:

> But how relevant is all this to would-be disciples . . .? A fo-
> cus so exclusively on the three years of Jesus' ministry in first
> century Palestine surely makes the whole matter much more
> remote to today.[5]

The truth is that asking about what discipleship meant to the
first disciples only takes us so far. We have managed to map
something of the start of the journey but we still have a long

---

5 Dunn, *Jesus' Call to Discipleship*, p. 122.

way to travel. In order to begin to answer our core question – What does it mean to follow Jesus today? – we need to know whether discipleship was the same or took different forms over time. Here again the New Testament has some answers for us.

Q2: Is Christian discipleship always the same?

Much work has been done on the New Testament to explore discipleship. Some of it, like that of James Dunn, has reconstructed for us a glimpse of the original preaching of Jesus and first disciples' response. Other writers have concentrated on the ways discipleship is portrayed in each of the Gospels and the other writings of the New Testament. In so doing, the question for them is: What did discipleship mean to the second generation of Christians? What did it mean to follow Jesus for those who heard of his death and resurrection through the preaching of the apostles and other missionaries and who were trying to live this out 30, 50 or even 100 years after the first Easter?

   The Gospels were clearly written for these disciples. Ernest Best, the New Testament scholar who made an extensive study of discipleship in Mark's Gospel, wrote that Mark's 'primary objective was pastoral: to build up his readers as Christians and show them what discipleship is'.[6] Likewise, Richard Longenecker writing about Luke's Gospel and the book of Acts says: 'For in analysing how he treats his sources we are often confronted with data that indicates quite clearly not only how Luke wanted his readers to respond to the questions "Who is Jesus?" but also how he wanted them to answer the question "What does it mean to be a follower of Jesus?".'[7]

---

   6 Ernest E. Best, *Following Jesus: Discipleship in the Gospel of Mark*, Journal for the Study of the New Testament, Supplement Series 4, Sheffield: JSOT, 1981, p. 12.

   7 Richard N. Longenecker (ed.), *Patterns of Discipleship in the New Testament*, Mcmaster New Testament Studies, Grand Rapids and Cambridge: Eerdmans, 1996, p. 50. The same is argued for Matthew and John. See Longenecker (ed.), *Patterns of Discipleship*, chapters 2 and 4. See also Fernando F. Segovia, *Discipleship in the New Testament*, Philadelphia: Fortress Press, 1985.

So how do the different Gospel writers depict discipleship and do they give the same answer?

Mark's picture of discipleship

Mark is a good place to begin. It is the oldest of the Gospels and most scholars agree that Matthew and Luke knew Mark's Gospel when they wrote, for they used his material extensively, sometimes retaining the way Mark presents it and at other times adding to or changing Mark's record.

According to Best, the key to understanding discipleship in Mark's Gospel is the central passage 8.22—10.52. This section is bounded by the healings of two blind men: the man healed in two stages and the healing of Bartimaeus. In the first healing, the man's sight is gradually restored. At the initial touch he can only see men as trees. It is only after a second touch that he sees clearly. This seems to be a metaphor for the disciples in the following chapters. They appear to see (that Jesus is the Messiah, 8.29) but do not see clearly (Peter cannot accept the Messiah as suffering, 8.32). They need a second touch to help them see the truth. At the end of the section Bartimaeus is healed straightforwardly and, what is more, he follows Jesus 'on the way'. This is a phrase used to indicate the way of discipleship.[8] Bartimaeus sees clearly and follows Jesus into Jerusalem, modelling true discipleship.

In the passages between the two healings Jesus predicts three times that he will suffer and be put to death and, following each prediction, there is some teaching about the nature of discipleship. The structure is a simple recurring pattern: (a) Jesus predicts his passion, then (b) there is an account of misguided behaviour or misunderstanding on the part of the disciples, and finally, this is followed by (c) Jesus' corrective teaching.[9] At each point the disciples are being led to a clearer idea of what it means to be a follower.

---

8 See Mark 8.27, 9.33, 10.32 and 10.52.

9 Larry W. Hurtado, 'Following Jesus in the Gospel of Mark – and Beyond', in Longenecker (ed.), *Patterns of Discipleship*, p. 12.

In this section the reader learns that a disciple:

- understands the significance of Jesus' death (8.31; 9.31–2; 10.34–5);[10]
- knows that following Jesus involves denial of oneself, active determination to follow, suffering and even death (8.34);
- must be prepared to let go of possessions (10.17–31);
- does not seek for rank and status but serves others (9.33–7; 10.35–45);
- belongs to an open and inclusive community (10.38–41);
- cannot set aside a marriage commitment (10.1–12);
- affirms women and children as significant persons (10.13–16 cf. 9.36–7).[11]

Some of these discipleship traits immediately strike us as the same or very close to what Dunn outlined for the earliest disciples: the openness of the community, the distraction of wealth (the reverse side of the kingdom for the poor) and the importance of respect for the marginalized. Other features are new or developed. In particular, we notice the teaching about marriage, which is slightly different from that of Matthew's record (Matthew 19.3–12); the teaching about true greatness being servanthood and the importance of understanding the meaning of Jesus' death. Other original features are slightly less emphasized. For example, there is no mention of sinners or tax collectors between chapter 8 and 10. These are mentioned in Mark chapter 2, where Jesus' ministry and opposition is recorded, but in relation to the core teaching about discipleship they are noticeable by their absence. What was almost certainly a central feature of the original call to discipleship is not passed on as a characteristic of the disciple to Mark's readers.

What we begin to discern in this the earliest Gospel is that there is a subtly changing understanding and expression of dis-

---

10 Best, *Following Jesus: Discipleship in the Gospel of Mark*, p. 13, suggests that Christology and soteriology imply a doctrine of the Christian life and an ecclesiology.

11 Hurtado, 'Following Jesus', pp. 14–15.

cipleship. It is consistent with the first call to follow Jesus and does not contradict it but discipleship is already developing and taking on new features.

This developing of the picture of discipleship is almost certainly related to the context in which Mark's readers find themselves. Best outlines the situation of Mark's church as based in Rome somewhere between AD 66 and 70, in a situation where persecution was known and might be threatening again. There is thus an apocalyptic atmosphere in the community (Mark 13) but this was not the dominant note. Rather, they – the readers – are struggling with issues that face them in the long wait for the second coming. No longer are they concerned with crossing barriers to sinners, for the community is made up of many who were formally outside the covenant. Instead, they are wrestling with issues concerning marriage, the nature of leadership, especially the desire of some of the members for positions of importance, and how to respond to the threat of persecution.[12]

Another vital point that Best notes about discipleship in Mark is the emphasis, in this Gospel, on Jesus leading and the disciples falling in behind. Best makes much of the Greek word '*proagein*', 'to go ahead' used at 10.32 where Jesus is said to be going ahead to Jerusalem. This word is used again at 14.28 when Jesus speaks of the cross, and again at 16.7 in the message given by the angel at the empty tomb. Best translates this 'going at your head'. For all the specific points about discipleship made by Mark in the section bracketed by the two healings, following the person of Jesus is the core. And this is not primarily following to death, though that might happen, but following the one who has gone beyond death: the risen Christ, who is always at the head of his people in mission. Disciples are to fall in behind Jesus on this pilgrimage of faith. Unlike disciples of other Rabbis, they will not become Rabbis; unlike teachers of philosophy, they will not themselves become teachers. They will always be disciples with Jesus as the Rabbi and teacher.

---

12 Best, *Following Jesus: Discipleship in the Gospel of Mark*, p. 9.

As such, they will imitate him in taking up the cross and denying themselves, in serving others rather than seeking status for themselves, in sustaining commitments such as marriage and in maintaining an open, respectful and inclusive community.

Mark thus maintains the emphasis that at the heart of discipleship is a following of Jesus. He transmits some of the core features of the original call to discipleship but draws out and develops other characteristics in relation to the context and challenges that this small church faces in Rome. The portrayal of what it means to follow Jesus is related both to the historical person of Jesus, his life, teaching, death and resurrection, and to the context and issues of Mark's church. In other words, the understanding of discipleship is being shaped by two forces – the person of Jesus and the tradition that is passed on about him, on the one hand, and the existential, practical and pressing issues of the contemporary world of those called to discipleship, on the other. We will see this even more clearly as we look at some other parts of the New Testament.

Discipleship in Luke and John

Luke and John seem to go in different directions from each other in what they emphasize about discipleship. The individual and distinctive characteristics and features of these two Gospels are widely known and acknowledged,[13] but what this conveys about discipleship is not often contrasted.

Where Luke puts additional stress on the poor and the dangers of wealth to discipleship, John hardly records anything about poverty[14] and none of Jesus' teaching about giving away one's wealth. Where Luke tells repeatedly of the good news for all and the inclusion of Gentiles, tax collectors, sinners, women and children, John put the emphasis on the disciples loving one

---

13 Longenecker (ed.), *Patterns of Discipleship*, p. 54.

14 The only reference to the poor in John is in relation to Jesus' anointing in chapter 12 where Judas complains that the perfume could have been sold and the money given to the poor. Jesus' response is to say that they will always have the poor with them but not always him.

another. While Luke retains the emphasis on the kingdom of God and fills out what it means, John only uses the phrase on one occasion and there it is not to do with good news for the poor, release for captives or sight for blind (Luke 4.14ff.) but to do with spiritual birth from above (John 3.3–5). Rather, John has Jesus making a series of statements about himself all beginning 'I am' (6.35; 8.12; 10.9; 10.11; 11.25; 14.6; 15.1) of which Luke seems to know nothing. For Luke discipleship means taking up the cross daily (notice the significant change from Mark 8.34); in John there is no mention of taking up the cross. The material peculiar to Luke (especially found in 'Luke's travel narrative', 9.51—19.27) stresses the virtues to be practised in discipleship, such as loving and helping others (10.25–37), persistence in prayer (11.5–13; 18.1–8), the importance of response to God (14.15–24), humility (18.9–14), concern for the lost (Luke 15), and shrewdness in one's affairs (16.1–12). In John the centre of discipleship is an intimate relationship with Jesus expressed in such images as the vine and the branches (John 15), and embodied in the 'beloved disciple' who at the Last Supper rests his head on the bosom of Jesus (John 13.23) just as Jesus rests in the bosom of God (John 1.18). Both Luke and John have an emphasis on the Holy Spirit but where in Luke the stress is on the empowering of the Spirit for mission and prophetic proclamation, the Spirit in John is the one to lead into truth, to remind disciples of Jesus' teaching, to convict the world of sin and to glorify Jesus. These two views of the Spirit are, of course, not exclusive but what is conveyed is different in tone and carries some divergent ideas about what it means to be a disciple. The overall pictures are sharply contrasting.

Suppose you only possessed one of these Gospels to guide your discipleship. If you had only Luke's Gospel you would think immediately that following Jesus was about mission and outreach, spreading the gospel far and wide and inviting everyone to receive the good news. Your following of Jesus would involve practical care for the poor, the marginalized and those in need. For this you would need to be a person of prayer, not distracted by possessions or wealth, with an empowering experience of the Holy Spirit, and, in taking up your cross daily, you would seek to nurture humility, compassion and obedience.

If you only had John's Gospel you might think that discipleship hinges on a personal relationship with Christ, knowing, believing and abiding in him. You would seek to practise loving others in the Christian community as a sign of belonging to Jesus and you would witness to Jesus as the one who came down from heaven and was raised high on the cross. You would be very conscious of being distinct and different from other groups, such as the disciples of John the Baptist, 'the Jews' and even secret or covert disciples of Jesus, for to be a true disciple is to know and openly confess that Jesus has come from the Father, whatever the consequences.

The reasons for these contrasting views of discipleship are manifold but a key factor is the life situation of the intended hearers. For the Gentile Christian readers of Luke the good news has spread throughout the whole world. As the end of the Acts of the Apostles suggests, the gospel is preached 'with all boldness and without hindrance' now in Rome, the centre of Empire and known world (Acts 28.31). The majority of Christians are Gentile rather than Jewish and the task of discipleship is to continue the missionary work that was undertaken by the apostles, and especially Paul. To do this requires commitment and the power of the Holy Spirit. It obliges people to sit light to wealth and possessions but hold tightly on to prayer, humility and concern for the lost. The questions that are uppermost for the first readers are to do with explaining to the growing Gentile Christian communities how to cross cultural boundaries, how to communicate the good news to Roman citizens and how to live on a day-to-day basis as Christians in the Roman Empire.

John's community, on the other hand, seems to reflect a time when Jewish Christians were expelled from the synagogue (John 9.22; 12.42 and 16.2) and thus the experience of these disciples is one of alienation from their roots – a small community faithful to Jesus cut adrift in a hostile environment. It is not surprising therefore to see Jesus portrayed as alien – one who came down from heaven – and was not received by his own (1.11). Disciples too are not of this world, they are born from above (3.7). The questions that they faced daily would be about how to relate to other Jews, how to continue a witness to the love of God, how to maintain a united community and to explain the offence taken by their former brothers and sisters at Jesus. Maybe too there were other faith groups, such as followers of John the Baptist, that continued (cf. Acts 18.25—19.5) and from which they wanted to distinguish themselves. The Gospel of John speaks to all these questions and suggests how the readers can practise the life of discipleship in their own time and place.

As with Mark, so in Luke and John we see that the picture of discipleship is shaped by two forces: the person of Jesus and the tradition that is passed on about him and the context and presenting issues of those disciples for whom the Gospel was written. In neither Luke nor John could we find evidence to accuse the writers of failing to pass on a tradition about Jesus or to make Jesus less than central. It may be that the Jesus of John is portrayed very differently from that of the Synoptic Gospels but there is no denying the cruciality to discipleship of the person of Jesus, his teaching, his death and resurrection. It is this living person who is followed. Discipleship is, in both accounts, however, related to the concerns and context of the readers. The good news is conveyed in a way that will help the second-generation disciples of their respective church communities practise their faith in the situations in which they find themselves.

The answer to our second question – Is Christian discipleship always the same? – is 'yes and no', according to the New Testament evidence. Yes, it is always focused on Jesus, his life and death and resurrection defining the locus of discipleship, but no, seemingly discipleship is never exactly the same in any two places and times. In some contexts the form and practice of discipleship can be radically different from others.

Hydrangea plants have the remarkable property of being able to change the colour of their flowers dramatically. A hydrangea with pink flowers transplanted to another soil may produce blue flowers where the pink ones had been before. Apparently this change depends on the soil conditions, in particular the amount of aluminium available in the earth in which it is planted. There is a bio-chemical synthesis between the elements in the new ground and the basic life of the plant that produces a radical colour change – so much so that at first encounter you might think it was different plant. Of course, if you looked carefully you would see that the shape of the flower petals and structure of the flower was more or less identical on the plant in either soil even though the overall view would be spectacularly changed. This analogy works well for what we see happening in different portrayals of discipleship in the New Testament. The commitment to follow Jesus who lived, died and rose again is the constant, like the structure of the flowers at the heart of the plant, but the pattern discipleship is fashioned by the setting, just as the shape and colour of the bush changes according to new soil into which it is planted.

Another metaphor for these changing patterns of discipleship is that of a dialogue or conversation. In an open conversation with many different voices and views, there is much exchange and no doubt some disagreement. But often when people are committed to the group and their common task there emerges from the conversation, by a process of careful listening and responding to convictions, an apparently new set of ideas or shared conventions by which to live. The new way of speaking and acting guards and respects the ideas brought to the conversation and yet provides a creative and authentic way forward. The dialogue about discipleship that we discerned at work in Mark's Gospel is even more pronounced when we compare the Gospels of John and Luke. The conversation between the contexts of discipleship they faced and the tradition about Jesus that they carried to it results in very different practices and patterns.

So the nature of discipleship does change, but can we know more about how this happens? It is time to turn to our third and final question.

Q3: How was discipleship worked out in new places and times?

We have identified the importance of dialogue in forging authentic discipleship. In order to explore the nature of this dialogue a little further, we will examine one other New Testament book: the Epistle to the Hebrews.

Discipleship in the Epistle to the Hebrews: A case study

As has been pointed out in several places, Hebrews is perceived as difficult and is not well read. [15] Despite this, it is a fascinating and insightful book and has a message about discipleship for its readers. The context of the letter or homily appears to be a Christian community that is tired and weary and tempted to give up because of the pressures – perhaps including organized persecution – that are weighing upon it. Usually dated around the mid 60s AD, its location is probably a small urban house-church, linked to the Jewish quarter of the city with roots in a Hellenistic synagogue, whose members are familiar with Jewish scriptures. [16] There is something of a leadership crisis, in that the leaders who first preached to them the word of God are now deceased (13.6), the current leaders are perhaps not respected (13.17), and the members seem to have little desire to have contact with outsiders (5.12). They may well want to retreat to a form of faith that is less prone to attract attention and difficulty for them – perhaps returning to the synagogue. [17] There is some evidence of members defecting (10.25) and of attraction to new, fanciful teaching (13.8). The questions for these Christians are to do with whether they have taken the right path,

---

15 N. T. Wright, *Following Jesus: Biblical Reflections on Discipleship*, London: SPCK, 1994, p. 3. William L. Lane, 'Standing before the Moral Claim of God: Discipleship in Hebrews', in Longenecker (ed.), *Patterns of Discipleship*, p. 222.

16 See William L. Lane, *Word Biblical Commentary, Volume 47a: Hebrews 1–8*, Dallas, Texas: Word Books, 1998.

17 See T. W. Lewis, in *New Testament Studies* 22 [1975–6], pp. 91–3 on the possible use of Isaiah 26.20.

whether to return to the Jewish rather than Jewish–Christian view of the world, how to find the truth in the scriptures, how to find the resources to face trouble and to resist their temptation to find an easier way.

How does the writer address this situation, these disciples and their questions? To what does he point them and what does he tell them about the nature of discipleship?

The broad answer is that he paints a fresh picture of Jesus. You notice the direction from the opening verses.

Long ago God spoke to our ancestors in many and various ways by the prophets, but in these last days he has spoken to us by a Son, whom he appointed heir of all things, through whom he also created the worlds. He is the reflection of God's glory and the exact imprint of God's very being, and he sustains all things by his powerful word. When he had made purification for sins, he sat down at the right hand of the Majesty on high, having become as much superior to angels as the name he has inherited is more excellent than theirs. (Hebrews 1.1–2)

The claim made is that the final and complete revelation was in Jesus (though the name is held back in the epistle until 2.9). He is the exact imprint of God – there is nothing closer and nothing carries the character of God more perfectly. This Son is the one through whom God created and sustains the world and it is he who has made the sacrifice for sin.

Thus, he sets forth a grand and decisive picture of Jesus. He then fills out this picture and reinforces its central point by a series of comparisons and categories. In chapter 1 the Son is declared to be superior to angels. In chapter 2 the idea of the earth as subject to human beings is raised then shown to be misleading because it clearly is not subject to human control. Rather, it is subject to Jesus (named here at 2.9) who, for a time, was made lower than the angels but is now crowned with glory and honour. In chapter 3 Jesus is shown to be greater than Moses and then from the end of chapter 4 until chapter

10, Christ is presented as the true and eternal priest – after the order of Melchizedek – who offered the sacrifice that takes away sin and thus made a new covenant.

Alongside this constellation of images – the revelation of God, creator and sustainer of the world, high priest and king at the right hand of God, crowned with glory and honour – the writer also adds the new title 'pioneer' or 'champion' (2.10) of the faith who came to lead his brothers and sisters and has already won the victory. This title is picked up again in the finale of his argument (12.2), as he points his reader-disciples to the faith and perseverance of Israel's heroes in the past and to Jesus who is the most important – the pioneer and champion. They are warned at a number of places what the consequence of giving up would be (3.12–15; 6.4–8; 10.26–31; 12.14–17, 25–9) but more importantly they are urged to fix their eyes on Jesus and run the race before them to the very end. Because Jesus is the champion, he is leading his people and, as high priest, he can sympathize with their trials and sufferings (4.15). Being alongside them he can enable them to live faithful lives of discipleship that manifest holiness. Their day-to-day living should be marked by provoking one another to love and good works and regularly meeting together (10.24–5), being open and vulnerable in practising hospitality (13.1), pursuing peace with everyone (12.14), giving thanks and praise to God (12.28 and 13.15), caring for those in prison, honouring marriage, supporting their leaders, doing good and sharing what they have (13.16).

The picture of Jesus then, strange as it may seem to modern readers, was of supreme importance in stimulating these early Christians to fresh faith and active discipleship. The fact that the epistle was recorded and passed on, suggests that its impact was significant and it was counted by the early Church as a model of Christian teaching. The author manages to connect the presentation of Christ with the lives of the readers, addressing directly their temptation to give up and lose heart and at the same time showing what Christian lives must be like to reflect commitment to this faith.

The way in which he arrives at this picture of Jesus is also of significance for it is here that we find some more clues to understanding the dynamic business of discipleship.

Method in Hebrews

The picture of Jesus is built from a variety of sources and ideas. First, the writer digs deep into the (Jewish) scriptures. Clearly much of the argument of the text of Hebrews is expository. That is, the author takes various scriptures and expounds them. In doing so he visits texts that are referred to nowhere else in the New Testament. In particular, he uses several Psalms (95.7–11; 110.4; 40.6–8) and Jeremiah 31.31.[18] Also he uses the rather obscure figure of Melchizedek, only mentioned in the Bible outside Hebrews at Genesis 14.18 and Psalm 110.4. The reason for choosing this figure seems to come from a need to portray Jesus as both king and priest. Normally this would be impossible because kings and priests were from different Jewish family lines. Jesus, as from the line of David, has the right kinship to be a royal, but by the same token was not qualified to be seen as a priest. But, argues the writer, it has happened before, for one of the two texts declares Melchizedek is a king (Genesis 14.18) and the other salutes him as a priest (Psalm 110.4). What is more, the latter also implies an eternal priesthood, which fits the person and work of Jesus well. This mining of the tradition provides insights, resources and possibilities to present a fresh picture of Christ.

Second, he employs ways of thinking that would have been current in the audience's culture to develop and make his ideas clear to his listeners. This is particularly evident in the use of the notion 'shadow and reality' by which he contrasts the earthly and heaven sanctuaries (8.5; 9.24) in which the true high priest made the once for all sacrifice (see from 4.14 onwards). One – the earthly one – is a mere shadow or type of the other – the heavenly, true and eternal reality. This kind of thinking, drawn

---

18 Lane, 'Standing before the Moral Claim of God: Discipleship in Hebrews', p. 221.

from Plato, would be familiar to many people in the first century and was used by others to interpret scriptural texts. The
writings of the Jewish writer Philo of Alexandria also used this
approach.

Third, he offers what Tom Wright calls 'a new reading of the
Old Testament'.[19] In a variety of ways, the writer presents the
Hebrew scriptures as an unfinished story that requires a final
chapter. The final chapter is Jesus himself and thus all the old
Scriptures can only make sense when read in the light of the
final chapter. This hermeneutical lens is another feature of this
presentation. Jesus, as the final revelation, must be the key to
unlock the meaning of all that was previously written.

Finally, he adds some creativity of his own. You could say
that all the above is the faith-driven creativity, weaving together
many previously unnoticed texts, contemporary ideas and a
new way of reading the scriptures. But he goes further taking a
word that hearers would immediately link with divine heroes
of the Hellenistic as well as the Jewish world. The origins of
the word 'champion' are hard to trace but it would have had
associations with such figures as Hercules, who wrestled with
death.[20] Here there is a link to an image of popular culture that
would have evocative resonances for his audience. This too is
utilized to effect in his portrayal of Jesus.

This fresh picture of Jesus reorients the Christians of this
community towards God and grounds their discipleship in
a contemporary Christology – one that speaks cogently to
their situation and the dilemmas and temptations they face.
The practices of discipleship that they are urged to adopt and
persevere with – growing in love and good works, offering
hospitality, visiting prisoners, honouring marriage, supporting
leaders, sharing resources, meeting together for worship – are
related to faith in Jesus the pioneer, champion, priest and king.
In other words, the dialogue between the tradition about Jesus
and the current context, gives rise not only to an articulation

---

19 Wright, *Following Jesus: Biblical Reflections on Discipleship*.
20 Lane, *Word Biblical Commentary, Volume 47a: Hebrews 1–8*.

of a pattern of discipleship, but also to a re-imagining of the person and work of Jesus and this in turn illuminates and calls forth the discipleship required of these believers.

This brief exercise on the Epistle to the Hebrews suggests that there is a pattern of working that is related to the nature of discipleship. The two forces that we noticed in the Gospels – the centrality of the person of Jesus and tradition about him and the contexts and issues of contemporary discipleship – are present also in this epistle and they are in dialogue. The writer, in an endeavour to present what following Jesus means for his audience, has to be active in facilitating this dialogue. He digs deeply into the tradition, which he reads through Christ-centred eyes. He engages with the contemporary culture, from which he utilized common notions and ways of thinking to convey his thoughts, and he is both bold and creative in his metaphors and images. As a result, a picture of Jesus and an outline of discipleship emerge. Both of these are in some ways new or fresh. He interprets anew who Jesus is and what he calls for from his disciples.

Discipleship as dynamic conversation

Although we have portrayed the work here as being of one person – the writer of the Epistle to Hebrews – it reflects something broader going on. Behind the work of this author, indeed the atmosphere in which he and this small group of Christians live, is a continual conversation between various voices. We can imagine this as a group of people around a table deeply engaged in dialogue with each other. One represents the convictions and writings of the Hebrew scriptures, another is the voice of popular cultural, while a third is telling the story of Jesus that she heard in her youth in a place across the sea, told originally in another language. Finally, there is one who relates the day-to-day problems of being a Christian in this place – the pressures, the opposition, the persecution, the despondence of the congregation. They have shared a meal together and now they converse at some length. As they talk, deep into the night, each one puts forward what she or he knows well and believes deeply and all share the struggle to find the way forward. How are they to make sense of this situation? What is it that God requires of them? What should they encourage or challenge each and the wider congregation to do as followers of Jesus? At various points they pray because they want to keep close to the one who is present but unseen. Then they continue in their conversation and seemingly from nowhere, in the early hours of the morning, one and then another offers images and ideas and new ways of reading the scripture that excite and energize them. They almost tumble over each other as they find words and actions to express their faith afresh. They hold up for one another a new and inspiring picture of their Lord and they see clearly what following him means.

If you have ever been in one of these conversations, you will recognize both the dynamics and the energy in this story. In a diagrammatic form it might look as like this.

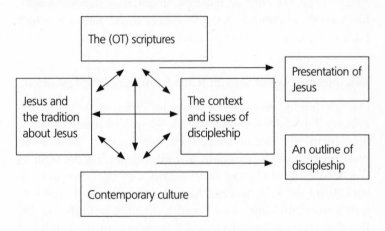

The cluster of two-headed arrows at the heart of the diagram conveys visually the nature of the conversation going on. It is a complex, critical and creative conversation between the tradition and the context of contemporary disciples. Within this conversation attention is giving to the wider tradition in which the person and story of Jesus is set and to the cultural thought forms of the present day. In each part of the conversation, as with any conversation, there is the possibility that views are confirmed, extended, developed or changed. This is not simply looking for a clever means of saying the old things in new and exciting ways. The context may be challenged and changed by the tradition and the tradition may be reformed and renewed in the fresh telling for new disciples in a particular context. This does not mean anything goes and theology can be invented from nothing. Nowhere is it possible to have anything or anyone other than Jesus – crucified and risen – at the very centre of discipleship but how one articulates the person of Jesus and the calling of discipleship can vary greatly from one context to another. The themes that we identified in the original call of Jesus by the Sea of Galilee – responding to God's kingdom, good news and compassion for the poor, humility, openness to the marginalized, costly service of others, love for one's neighbour and the practice of forgiveness – will appear again and again. They are core convictions, foundational benchmarks. But even these are only part of a bigger conversation in which faith is worked out in the practice of discipleship.

Discipleship: What we can learn from the New Testament

Discipleship means different things for different groups of followers of Jesus represented in the New Testament. For the first disciples it meant being with and assisting Jesus in his proclamation of the kingdom of God, celebrating the signs of God's rule and declaring the good news to the poor and sinners. It meant also hearing the call and calling on others to turn around, to trust in God and to live life in faith. For the first disciples, discipleship would be redefined by the death and resurrection of Jesus and this propelled them into proclaiming Jesus as the focus and agent of God's rule, making faith in him central. For second-generation Christians, discipleship means a variety of beliefs, actions and practices. For Mark's readers the core of discipleship is connected with understanding the death of Christ, self-denial and costly service as disciples followed Jesus. For Luke and John discipleship has different vectors: for the former it is a discipleship fit for an outward moving missionary endeavour with an accent on the poor and the marginalized; for the latter its orientation is inwards to the quality of the relationships between the disciple and Jesus and the disciples connections with one another. In the Epistle to the Hebrews, the complexity of process of discerning the discipleship response is apparent, as it involves not only a process directly linked to the issues the community faces but also a rediscovery and refashioning of traditions about Jesus, through the reading of the scriptures and engagement with culture.

It is thus not possible to extrapolate an unchanged content of discipleship. There are no uniform practices or set of values that consistently mark it out and, while there are some features that can be ruled out as never being associated with discipleship in the New Testament, such as acting violently or deceitfully, and there are recurring characteristics and hallmarks, such as loving, forgiving and serving others, it is difficult to set out the characteristics of discipleship for every disciple in every place.

We have one clear fixed focus, however. In all the New Testament writings it is the person of Jesus who is the centre and focus of discipleship. All writers agree that how you see and respond to Jesus is critical. He is the one who lived and taught, died on the cross and rose from the dead. However his story is told and his picture portrayed, he is the key to the meaning of life and the ways of God and direct response to him is required. Like Mark's disciples, those who come afterwards are to see the living Jesus proceeding at the head and to follow him.

We perhaps should not expect discipleship to be a question of simply passing on a fixed collection of traditions and practices. As Martin Hengel[21] has pointed out, the following of Jesus is distinct from the idea of the ancient Rabbi with his pupils or the Greek philosopher with his learners. The job of those disciples is to pass on intact the tradition of the teacher or school. They must learn it by rote and hand on without addition or fault. For the followers of Jesus the goal is not passing

---

21 Hengel, *The Charismatic Leader and His Followers.*

on an untainted tradition but the following of a person, vibrant in the midst of life with all its joy, suffering and sorrow.

Rather than take a set of unchanging content or practices we are offered something more dynamic and demanding. Alongside the centrality of commitment to Jesus Christ, we see in the New Testament a pattern of conversation between our faith commitment, our inherited tradition and our present-day context and issues. It is by entering ourselves into this living conversation that we become disciples. Some of the elements that facilitate this living conversation are apparent to us. We see a need to dig deep into the tradition(s) that we have received, to read them critically and creatively and to be open to their readings of us. We perceive too a need to engage with the context and culture of our own time and place, to understand as far as we can the ideas and thought forms that dominate our culture and to read these also both critically and creatively, open to their ability to give us insight into God and even disclose things of God that may cause us to re-read our traditions. In all this we have the responsibility not only to follow Jesus but to make him known and in the setting forth of a picture of Jesus for our own age we may also discover the nature of discipleship and know for ourselves what following Jesus means.

In David Brown's book on discipleship the core argument is that discipleship cannot be read off from the scriptures as a simple learning exercise. Rather discipleship is a living process that recognizes what the scriptures are saying and also how our own context is different.

> Discipleship is thus both a matter of locating ourselves within Jesus' story and acknowledging the way in which our own situation differs significantly from his. Christian discipleship needs to be aware of these differences if it is not to make impossible demands upon the scriptures or judge later developments by the wrong criteria.[22]

22 David Brown, *Discipleship and Imagination: Christian Tradition and Truth*, Oxford: Oxford University Press, 2000, p. 8.

It is only by looking carefully at our own context and issues, by re-examining our picture of God and by re-engaging with the traditions of God we receive, that a dialogue of discipleship can occur. The dialogue is of the essence of discipleship. You can't stand outside this dialogue and observe it – for the God who has been made known in Jesus is in the midst of the dialogue, and God is to be discovered there. Only by entering into and engaging in these conversations can we find the truth of God and hope to follow him faithfully. This may well be the New Testament's core message about discipleship.

2

The Context of Our Discipleship

For many years I made the same mistake every time I visited Leeds. Because I grew up there I thought I knew the city, its shops, its streets, its markets, its theatres, its one-way systems, its car parks, its train and bus routes, its back streets and its danger areas. I knew where to go to see a film, or play tenpin bowling, to eat a good meal or to meet friends. I even knew where to cross the busiest road safely and where to drink Chinese tea. Of course, the longer I lived away from the city the less it resembled what I remembered. Its buildings and streets changed, shops closed and new ones opened. Cinemas, theatres, indeed the whole city's entertainment industry, were redefined. The roads, rail and bus systems were radically changed. The result was that on visits to see family, although I confidently thought I knew where I was going and what I was doing, I got lost over and over again and even if I found where I wanted to go, it no longer looked or felt the same.

Followers of Jesus in early twenty-first century Britain find themselves in a very strange landscape compared with those of previous generations. Even Christian disciples of only 50 years ago would, if transported forward through time to today, meet changes that they had not anticipated. I don't mean by that simply the new wind farms, mobile-telephone masts, multiplex cinemas, vast shopping centres or internet terminals in cafés, banks, airports and homes, all of which proliferate in our present environment. There are deeper changes at the beginning of the twenty-first century, which impinge upon those who seek to be disciples: cultural changes that have accompanied, underlie or are the result of, the architectural, scientific and physical changes around us. These intellectual shifts have profoundly altered the way people think, act and relate and thus form a new and complex context for discipleship. In this chapter we will outline these major changes and identify some of the issues they raise for disciples.

Disoriented disciples

George is 67. He has been a Christian for over 50 years, and even before he committed himself to the faith he belonged to a Christian family and went first to Sunday school and then to church with his parents. He has lived and worked in the same town for the whole of his life and during that time he has moved churches three times, on each occasion because the congregation had grown too small to be viable and so joined with another church of the same denomination. He used to be active in several of the church's activities: Bible study, men's fellowship and prayer breakfast. He was also involved in his trade union and saw his union activity as part of his Christian duty. He would occasionally offer a word to witness to his workmates. He no longer speaks about God much. At best he can talk about the Church, what it was like and what it ought to be like. Saying grace at meals, which was once a family ritual, has died in his family, as his children and grandchildren seems to be less connected to Christian faith. He does not engage much with the Bible, apart from hearing it read in church, and he is no longer involved in the weekly meetings at church. He wonders sometimes now if he has been faithful and whether the decline in the church life is, in part, his fault. He attends Sunday worship regularly still, gives his money and tries to show kindness and friendship to the church members. There is much talk from the minister at church about new ways of being church, but it is hard for George to imagine what these might be – it sounds very different and unfamiliar. He wonders what God wants him to do now?

Mary is 36 years old. She has a wide circle of friends built up from school, college, work and from contacts through her children. She belongs to a growing evangelical Anglican church and is actively involved in a cell group and some youth work. Hers is a 'conventional marriage' with the wedding taking place in church as she and her husband are both committed Christians. However, many of her friends have cohabited, seemingly happily, and don't show any inclinations to get married. At some of her 'girls' nights' the talk is often of yoga with a few spending a good deal of money on special weekends and even week-long courses away. It is clear from the conversation that there is a 'spiritual' dimension to these courses and she is unsure how to react to this and what to say about her friends' lifestyles.

Michael is 29. He became a Christian only two years ago through participating in an Alpha course. The course was great, lots of discussion and good food and insights into Jesus and Christian faith. The church has been welcoming but he misses the level of engagement with the faith and others that was so much a part of the course. He has been asked to help in a new Alpha course and he has been praying about whom to invite. The persons who most come to mind are a couple from university days. The problem is that they are actively gay. They are very open to talk about Christian faith and he thinks they might respond positively to an invitation to the course. He is not so sure that the church community will be as open to them as they are to exploring the spiritual dimension of life. He admires his friends whose love and care for each other is real and deep and he wonders what inviting them to consider Christianity will mean for them.

Min Ho is from Korea. He moved to the UK about eight years ago. He works for a large international company and is in middle management in its UK base. He worships at a Korean church that uses a building also used by a United Reformed Church but otherwise the two Christian congregations have very little contact. He likes the church because it keeps him connected with his native language and culture and it offers support to a number of families based in the UK, mainly for children's education often with absent fathers supporting them financially from Korea. He is aware that his faith and his culture are closely linked but that his work seems to operate in a different world altogether. Most of the time this is fine, it allows him to keep different parts of his life separate and concentrate on each in turn. He is making good progress in his career and helping to win many Korean families for the church. Occasionally, however, he has doubts about whether compartmentalizing his life in this way means that he is like two people rather than one.

Last year *Hannah* married Rajit. She is a committed Christian. He is a devout Hindu. They are very much in love and encourage each other in their faiths. Her Christian friends, however, have been mixed in their reaction. Some have been delighted that Rajit is a person of faith whereas others have been very unsure that such a marriage could work. Some advised privately that she should not marry a non-Christian and others have said that Hannah should be seeking to convert her husband. What will they do if and when children come along? Hannah has a sense that God is at work in both their lives and feels talk about conversion is insulting. She thinks that being a disciple of Jesus is not incompatible with her marriage but she is unsure whether the Church shares her view.

Louise's parents moved from Jamaica to London in the 1970s. They joined an Anglican church that was welcoming and is now a thriving, largely black church congregation. She has felt the call of God on her life and trained as a youth worker with a view to working for the church. People have suggested that she might be called to be a priest, though becoming friends with their female curate Louise has shown her how hard it can be for women in leadership in the Church. On gaining a distinction in her course she began applying for youth work jobs about a year ago but so far has not been offered a post. She suspects that this may be connected with her gender and her ethnicity but, of course, this has never been said in any of the job interviews or visits. Several of her non-Christian friends have experienced prejudice too but they say to her 'at least we are not trying to work for an institution that pretends to be about justice but continues to discriminate on the basis of skin colour and sex'. She wonders how to respond to this kind of comment.

Sign-posts

These stories represent how some of the changes of the last 50 years have impacted on particular Christian disciples and what issues it has raised for them. Let us look at some of these changes in more detail, put names to them and tease out further the implicit challenges they contain for disciples seeking to follow Jesus. For convenience, we examine our cultural shifts under three headings:

- Post-national.
- Post-modern.
- Post-christendom.

Post-national

This week I heard that a couple I know are expecting their second child. The mother is from Norway and the father from the south-east of England. Their first child was born as they moved from Norway to England last year and, as they look forward to the new addition to the family, they are considering the possibility of working in Holland. If they decide to take the appointment, it is likely that their second child will be born shortly after they arrive. Between the four family members it is quite possible that they will have passports from three different countries.

While this may not be everybody's experience, many people will have friends or family members whose lives are increasingly lived like this. When I left home at 18 to study, I was the first person from either side of my family to have moved out of the Leeds–Bradford conurbation for several generations by choice (according to our family history there were some earlier ones who were sent to prison elsewhere!). What is more, after studying, marrying someone from the midlands and then working in different parts of Britain, it has become almost impossible to locate our identity in one place. Whereas my parents, grandparents and great grandparents would have proudly identified themselves as being 'Yorkshire born and Yorkshire bred', coming from Yorkshire was and is only part of the way I see myself. My children are now at the stage of nearing the end of study and seeking careers. The jobs they are considering are in almost any part of Europe or North America and they have not ruled out South East Asia, Africa or Australasia. It may be that in a few years' time they will see coming from Britain only as a part of their identity.

People now move not only to another town or city but to other countries and continents. *The Independent* front page on 16 Nov 2007 carried a headline 'Migration Watch' with the summary strap line 'Astounding new figures show record numbers of migrants are crossing the world in search of better lifestyles. Should they be welcomed? Are they parasites? Or should they all go back where they came from?' It was a clever way to draw in the prejudices of some readers, who might assume that this referred to those coming to Britain from other parts of the world, whereas in fact it referred to the large number of UK citizens moving abroad. According to the Office of National Statistics almost a million people moved into or out of Britain in 2006, a little less than 2 per cent of the UK population. Of these, some 207,000 UK nationals left to live permanently in other countries, another 193,000 foreigners returned home after settling in this country for a time and 591,000 people from other parts of the world settled here. These are official statistics and are, thus, likely to underestimate the movements of people to and from Britain. According to a BBC survey in 2007 over 13 per cent of adults hope to move abroad in near future.

This is not solely a British experience. Migration occurs on a large scale in various parts of the world, making the world smaller and more diverse and with consequent implications for identity. Richard Tiplady paints a graphic picture of this diversity in his portrayal of scenes at the football world cup finals in June 2002 with Italian–Americans getting up at 3 a.m. and making their way to an Italian café in New York's Greenwich village to watch the televised match between Italy and Croatia while, 5,000 miles away, scores of inhabitants in Soweto crowded around a small screen to watch South Africa play Paraguay and in Paris hundreds of Senegalese danced jigs in front of the Arche de la Défense when Senegal vanquished their former colonial masters 1–0.[1]

You don't have to move to another part of the world, however, to sense the cross-border nature of modern life. Overseas tourism to and from the UK is a booming business. The number of visits to North America made by Brits each year is now around 4.8 million, with a further 54.6 million visiting other European destinations and 10.2 million travelling to other parts of the world, while visits by overseas residents to the UK is over 32 million.[2] Likewise, around 800,000 British households now own a second residence abroad, a staggering 45 per cent increase between 2004 and 2006, and thus make regular visits to holiday or live for the part of the year in another country. On the home front, apparently the most popular meal ordered in UK restaurants is now chicken tikka masala[3] and there are colourful Chinatowns to be found in London, Liverpool, Manchester, Newcastle, Sheffield, Belfast and Glasgow.

I have termed this phenomenon 'post-national' despite the fact that the term is not widely used. The preferred word is 'globalization', though there are various different and contested meanings given to globalization and some hear the

---

1 Richard Tiplady, *World of Difference: Global Mission at the Pick and Mix Counter,* Carlisle: Paternoster, 2003.

2 Figures for 2007. Source: ONS website: http://www.statistics.gov. uk/

3 Tiplady, *World of Difference.*

undertones of post-colonial western imperialism in the term.[4] To speak of globalization can easily conjure up the spectre of large multi- or trans-national companies taking advantage of (or exploiting) the cheapest labour available, international capital movements that avoid tax and the exporting of western fast food, fashion and electronics with the consequent cultural and commodity restrictions, the perpetuation of poverty, and the erosion of local diversity. Clearly it would be irresponsible to pretend that there is no truth in these concerns but they do not represent the whole picture. What is happening seems to involve, indeed may be driven by capitalist forces, but there are significant other features that suggest that a good deal more is going on than trade (fair or unfair). As well as the stretching of economic and political activities across frontiers, commentators stress the speed of communication so that people and ideas as well as capital and products travel faster than ever before, the increasing impact of distant events so that local events can have global consequence, and the intensification of interconnectedness, which some have called a global consciousness. Jan Scholte summarizes globalization as a 'major reconfiguration of social geography'. In other words, the rapid movement of goods, services and people around the world and the meeting and mixing up cultures which has accompanied it makes us think, act and relate to each other in a profoundly different way. This is indeed a 'new world in which we live'.

Gains and losses of post-nationalism

Aspects of this global village have undoubtedly enhanced our experience. We have already noted the variety of food that is now available to us from all parts of the world and with a huge variety of styles of cooking. There are cultural festivals in our localities and, increasingly, film, art, literature and music from

---

4 Emmanuel Y. Lartey, *Pastoral Theology in an Intercultural World*, Peterborough: Epworth, 2006, expresses a preference for 'internationalisation' for this reason. See Jan Aart Scholte, *Globalization: A Critical Introduction*, Basingstoke: Macmillan, 2000.

around the globe is accessible to us. Hosts as well as immigrants are enriched by mutual contact and honest exchange. A few years ago *Time Together*, the refugee mentoring scheme,[5] was set up to bring volunteers to help refugees find their way in Britain. The volunteers as well as the refugees consistently witness to the enrichment of their lives through the friendship and the insights and experiences that came through the scheme. Likewise, the contacts between churches, gudwaras, temples and mosques, where developed, have often led to deeper understanding and appreciation from participants, way beyond their expectations.

The global nature of the world has also prompted new awareness. For example, world poverty has come onto the agenda in radically new ways in the last ten years with the 'Jubilee 2000', 'Drop the Debt', and 'Make Poverty History' campaigns and the fair trade and ethical trade movements. Likewise, we have become aware of climate change and damage done to the planet as a whole. Human rights work has become a key reference point for guarding the dignity and integrity of human persons.

But there are other aspects of post-nationalism that are unsettling. People who have forged a sense of identity through where they live and the traditions that are associated within their locality, are sometimes bewildered by the sheer range and diversity of the culture to which they now belong. This diversity does not simply relate to food and dress styles but also to patterns of family life, religious practice and political interests. There are choices to be made in the mixing of cultures that has grown out of globalization. The question of how far one persists with the traditions of one's background or adapts to live at ease with one's neighbours is felt by both hosts and immigrants. At a consumerist level, the range of ways of living in the world is extended and choice increased and there are now more ways of defining oneself than ever before and for individuals the question of truth claim versus social custom becomes more urgent.

---

5 See http://www.timetogether.org.uk/

Some features of globalization are sinister and threatening. Our complex interdependence creates an opaque wall that hides a multitude of activities and actions. In recent news incidents over 9 million toys made in China for the company Mattel had to be recalled because they did not meet the European and US safety standards.[6] Gap Clothes, a company with publicly stated ethical policies, discovered that some of its clothes, were being made by child labour in the Shahpur Jat area of New Delhi, India.[7] In both cases the companies producing the goods claimed that they had no knowledge of what happened in the process of making the products. Hiddenness goes hand in hand with a lack of accountability so that some billionaires operating on the world stage and reaping huge rewards pay little or no tax to any country. Similarly, pornography can be produced in ways that are hard to track down and perpetrators of the more exploitative and brutal material are not traceable or prosecutable. The environmental cost of travel and consumption is now more than ever known to us through global warming and ozone depletion but it is difficult to know how waste is being dealt with when countries and companies export rubbish for disposal in other nations, such as the Ivory Coast, though occasionally we learn of the effects when local people die of the resultant disease.[8]

Alongside all this, there is a sense of loss of control in the face of the grand scale of events and the distance between the places where decisions are made and the places that they impact. It is something of a British pastime to complain about decisions made in Brussels that tie the hands of the British parliament, and some politicians are not slow to exploit the fear of being taken over by European laws. Likewise, in the sphere of scientific research and experimentation what is not allowed in one country perhaps for moral or ethical reasons may be allowed, indeed encouraged, in another. Nation states themselves some-

---

6 David Ellis, CNNMoney.com, 15 August 2007.

7 Dan McDougall, *The Observer*, Sunday 28 October 2007.

8 *Independent*, 21 September 2006; see http://news.independent. co.uk/world/africa/article1640485.ece

times express feelings of impotence in the face of unregulated transnational companies and international financial markets and paralysis over, for example, ecological damage. It is now widely argued by political thinkers that international justice is struggling in the face of inappropriate or, worse still, structurally unfair international institutions[9] that ought to facilitate justice but instead do little or nothing to redistribute wealth,[10] and thus permit companies freedom to reek havoc on the world's poor.[11]

Perhaps the most feared dimension of globalization is the conflict and terrorism that has erupted in the early twenty-first century. 9/11 and 7/7 are dates now etched on the consciousness of most people in Britain and North America and these two countries are significantly committed in military terms to wars in several regions of the world and in the process contributing to constant nervousness at home about terrorist threats and racial conflicts. As David Clark has indicated, the globalization has disturbed, displaced and threatened local cultures and there are deep clashes of convictions and world views which will not easily be resolved.[12]

Issues for disciples

The issues identified above, namely loss of identity, anonymity, lack of control and fear of the unknown, translate into the ordinary day-to-day experience of disciples. George, for example, simply cannot imagine what new ways of being church might be, he is also fearful of this direction of change for it will

---

9 See T. Pogge, S. Caney, J. Stiglitz, R. Devetak and R. Higgott, 'Justice Unbound? Globalisation, States and the transformation of the social bond', *International Affairs*, 75: 3 (1999), pp. 483–98.

10 See C. Beitz, *Political Theory and International Relations*, Princeton: Princeton University Press, 1979.

11 Naomi Klein, *No Logo: No Space, No Choice, No Jobs: Taking Aim at the Brand Bullies*, London: Flamingo, 2000.

12 David Clark, *Breaking the Mould of Christendom: Kingdom Community, Diaconal Church and the Liberation of the Laity*, Peterborough: Epworth, 2005.

take him away from all that has shaped his identity to date. He also feels he has lost control of events that he could once influence and strangely guilty for the failure of the churches to which he belonged. Hannah has met and fallen in love with someone who has moved to work in the UK. She and her Christian friends are faced with a diversity of deeply held religious conviction and practice. Her Christian friends are fearful for Hannah's faith, the future of her family and their own truth claims. Min Ho holds on to his faith and his ethnic culture by keeping questions of integrated identity at bay and allowing two identities to flourish side by side.

Clearly post-nationalism puts many issues on the agenda for disciples. If it is God's world, disciples cannot be merely concerned with a domestic agenda. Issues of international justice, environmental responsibility, the relationship between different faiths and the creation of communities that can provide identity and safety while coping with great diversity, are all key issues. What is more, the deepening sense of the inter-relatedness of everything means these things can never be wholly someone else's concern. What I do or do not do has an impact elsewhere. That also means that world issues are my issues: plastic bags thrown carelessly away may end up choking dolphins. At the same time, all this has to be lived in the everyday worlds of ordinary disciples attempting to negotiate the new complex world on their doorstep. It is here that we are often most vulnerable, for the big picture issues feel even more messy and we feel more powerless in the intense and untidy melee of lived reality in our post-national mixed up communities.

Post-modernity

Post-modernity is the term given to the collection of attitudes, views and values that appear to have come to characterize the culture of western nations gradually over the last half century, together with the lifestyles that express them. The reason for the tag 'post' is that many of the aspects of this culture stand over against and depart from some of the characteristics of modernity, the culture growing from the Enlightenment and accompanying the age of science. Rather than suggesting that the modern period is finished, post-modernity seems to be voicing a series of critiques of some of the apparently confining and controlling discourse of modernity. Post-modern people are less convinced than their forbears that rationality is the key to human life and development; they are more suspicious of grand narratives and authority structures, whether these are produced by churches or scientific communities; they are more inclined to accept several ways of approaching and understanding truth and can live comfortably with diversity and difference, even contradiction. They are willing to blur boundaries and confuse categories. They are more inclined towards images and stories rather than scientific proof alone as ways of understanding the world and the self. They are not disposed to delay gratification of their desires for goods or services but want to experience things more immediately and are willing to live on credit and with debt.

Almost certainly the features of post-modernity have a resonance, if not a causal link, with some of the development of the late twentieth century. In particular, the development of the internet, with its easy access to vast amounts of information has strengthened the idea of knowledge as available to many rather than the few and thus reinforced the notion of flat rather than hierarchical structures. Its chat rooms and online games attract large numbers of people who wish to interact with each other on particular interests. The streaming of video and downloadable music, as well as text and pictures have enabled people to determine what and when they watch, listen and respond, in a similar way to the multi-channel TV and widespread availability of DVDs and computer games. Some of the most successful companies on the internet themselves embody the nature of post-modernity: eBay, for example, has been massively successful. In 1997 it was offering 800,000 online auctions per day with a 140 million hits per week and by 2006 it had 212 million registered users.[13] The reasons for its success are to do

13 William Gibson, *My Obsession* (http://www.wired.com/wired/ar-

with the flat market for buyers and sellers, its participatory experience buzz, the sheer size and range of goods on sale and the possibility of finding either specialist collectors' items or linking up with like-minded folk.

Another online development has been Wikipedia. When I was at school the definitive reference point and first port of call for any project was the *Encyclopaedia Britannica*. It resided in our local library in several volumes and was compiled by experts. Nowadays, looking up information is more likely to be done online and the first place many people begin their research is Wikipedia. It exists only online and is compiled by users. That is, articles that appear can be written by anyone and can be revised by other users who want to correct or update the information. Wikipedia is sometime criticized in academic circles for this very reason – how can one sure that the information is accurate and not written by a crank? – but on the whole it is reliable and, as most serious students will use it to get started on a topic rather than as the last and definitive word, it functions remarkably well: 268 million people visit the Wikipedia site every year. The symbolism here is important. In the modern period when knowledge was seen to be more settled and solely in the hands of experts, *Encyclopaedia Britannica* represented knowledge. In post-modern culture knowledge is seen as more fluid, more subjective, rapidly out of date and something to which all can make a contribution. Thus, Wikipedia is the symbol of knowledge.

Leonard Sweet describes post-modern people as EPIC.[14] This is an acronym for Experiential, Participatory, Image Driven, and Connected. People in post-modernity, he argues, are interested more in experience than in goods and services. He cites the evidence for this as the growth of the experience travel industry, and the orientation of industry towards selling experiences. As one senior company executive put it: 'Selling is not

---

chive/7.01/ebay.html: cf. (http://www.thebidfloor.com/ebay_facts.htm)

14 Leonard Sweet, *Post-Modern Pilgrims*, Nashville: BH Publishing, 2000.

about peddling a product. It is about wrapping a product in a service – and about selling both the product and the service as an experience.'[15]

Post-moderns are equally concerned to participate. Witness the growth of participatory TV shows and the decline (believe it or not) in TV watching among children and young people in favour of more interactive activities – interactive books, video-games and trying real-life experiences encountered through computers and TV. At the same time, the number of people designing their own weddings, funerals and other life events has dramatically risen.

Images drive not only advertising and internet sites but also the way people think and conceive the world and themselves. This visual conceptualizing fits post-modern ways of thinking because images are polyvalent and evoke emotions as well as conveying information. Finally, contrary to the individualism that seems to pervade consumerist culture, post-moderns want to connect with others, though their ways of connecting may now be of a different kind – via chat rooms (which account for 25 per cent of time spend on the internet): through mobile phones, texting and email and through new networks of people linked around particular interests.

The challenges of post-modernity

We have already met some of the strengths and challenges of post-modernity, for many of its characteristics and features are present in the post-national experience. New rapid forms of communication, enhanced visual imagery and large scale people movement have all helped bring about a heightened consciousness of diversity with the implications for identity and fear of the unknown. These aspects of the global connec-tivity that has brought about post-nationalism are intensified and developed when they become embedded in an overarch-ing culture. Thus, diversity in a cultural framework creates an

---

15 Marilyn Carlson Nelson quoted in Sweet, *Post-Modern Pilgrims*, p. 33.

inclination towards pluralism and relativism and underpins a suspicion of authority structures and stories. It encourages contextual explanations and supports situated morality and the cultivation of multiple identities. Likewise, the unprecedented high level of participation in all forms of media fuels a sense that experts can be challenged, whether they are identifying talent in the 'X Factor', giving an opinion on a current affairs discussion programme or holding forth on the ethics of genetic engineering in a chat room. The regular 'new scientific findings' reported in headline form on the news that tells that what was bad for health last year is good for health this year reinforces a suspicion of 'independent views', authority structures and meta-narratives. This hermeneutics of suspicion has become a deep cultural value because is it reinforced by numerous sources.

Issues for disciples

We see these characteristics in our 'disoriented disciples' stories. Mary and Michael are both uncomfortable in the face of the experience and lifestyles of their friends. Mary wonders what to make of her friends' involvement in yoga and their talk of spirituality. Is it what her church has described to her in the past as a false, even demonic, form of spirituality ultimately leading people astray or is it a genuine but different experience of the transcendent dimension, which she knows in another way? Should she seek to encourage her friends away from this path or affirm them and find common ground on which to share something of her own faith? She is sufficiently shaped by the post-modern suspicions of grand stories to know that the Church may not always get it right. Michael does not judge his gay friends solely on the basis of the received wisdom of the Church either. He knows that his church would be uncomfortable with an actively gay couple and he has heard the reasons given from the Bible why this is unacceptable, but he also approaches this through his personal knowledge of his friends. He believes he sees in them love and care lived out in a long-term committed relationship and recognizes this as authentic.

He wants them to know the deep joy of a faith in God that he has found but fears that this may destroy something beautiful in the process or be rejected by his friends because of the threat to their loving partnership.

Post-modernity is now well established as a culture in the western world and whether Christians like it or not it provides one of the contexts for discipleship. It will be a dialogue partner for the Church for some time to come and thus mission, worship and discipleship will be shaped out of the interaction of gospel, Church and post-modernity for the foreseeable future. Issues about truth claims and context, realism versus relativism, lifestyle and morality will be played out in the everyday lives of followers of Jesus living in a post-modern culture.

Post-Christendom

By the end of the twentieth century Britain was one of the most secular places that the world has ever known.[16]

This is the conclusion of the historian Callum Brown. The quotation comes from the last chapter of his book on religion and culture in twentieth-century Britain in which he charts what has happened to religion, especially Christianity, stage by stage over the last 100 years as Britain moved from a 'highly religious society' where 'nearly every person would claim some attachment to a religion' and 'very few with a faith were non-Christian' to a nation in which the Christian Church has few members, a falling attendance rate, little or no influence in civil society and is peripheral to the lives of most people.

There is no doubt, statistically, that church attendance has fallen dramatically and it appears to be a continuing declining prospect. Some denominations are predicted to disappear altogether before the middle of the century. Even though there is some evidence of growth in a number of churches, the overall picture is still one of a shrinking institution and with that a

---

16 Callum G. Brown, *Religion and Society in Twentieth-Century Britain*, Harlow, UK: Pearson, 2006, p. 317.

consequent reduction in resources of every kind. The age profile of churchgoers is heavily weighted towards the elderly, and while there was some hope that Generation X (people born between 1960 and 1980) might continue to show some interest in spirituality, the next generation appears not to share this hunger and it may indicate a decreasing interest in each successive generation.

More difficult to decide is whether Christian influence has declined. For Brown it is clear that it has.[17] The policies of successive governments have moved away from the intentions and aims of the churches on many moral issues and the churches have found themselves on the losing side of significant public debates. Popular literature, images and ideas from which people construct their self-understanding draw less and less on Christian sources. Others have argued that Christianity is going through a transition and that its influence continues to be strong but in new ways.[18]

This decline in the status and significance of the Church in Britain is part of what many authors have been describing for many years as the end of Christendom. This is quite simply the end of the era that began with the Emperor Constantine, who established Christianity as the official religion of the Roman Empire and ushered a period of wealth and influence for the church and a succession of forms of alliance between state and Christianity that ensured the continuance of power and authority for the Church. For over 1,600 years the Christian churches in Europe have existed where Christianity and belonging to church was the norm. Even for Christian dissidents or renewal movements the backdrop was a culture that assumed Christianity. This is now coming to a close. Although the gradual dismantling of Christendom has been going on for over 200

---

17 Callum G. Brown, *The Death of Christian Britain: Understanding Secularisation*, London: Routledge, 2001. See also S. Bruce, *God Is Dead: Secularisation in the West*, Oxford: Blackwell, 2002.

18 See for example Jane Garnett, Matthew Grimley, Alana Harris, William Whyte and Sarah Williams (eds), *Redefining Christian Britain: Post 1945 Perspectives*, London: SCM Press, 2006.

years, it was the second half of the twentieth century that saw the acceleration of the process and the deep separation of political structures and policies and popular culture from the life of the Church.

The implications of the end of Christendom are spelled out for the Church in many places. For one thing, there is simply less knowledge of Christianity. The language of Christian faith, the stories of the Bible and the activities of worship are unfamiliar to most. It is a minority language, only spoken by a few, and needs a lot of translating. A second implication is that the churches no longer set the agenda in public life or moral law. They have a decreasing right to a privileged opinion and must be one voice among many in the determining of public courses of action. Third, this relative weakness has allowed critics the opportunity to call to account the churches' use of power and privilege in the past. The 1960s TV programme 'That was the Week that Was' famously satirized religion in a way not previously known on television. Prior to that, along with royalty and political institutions, religion was protected by broadcasting prohibitions.[19] Since then, scandals of various kinds connected to churches have been exposed including extensive child sexual abuse and complicity in immoral acts of the past. It is a not a comfortable time to be a Christian!

The toxins of Christendom

Many Christian thinkers welcome a post-Christendom era. Earlier writers like John Wesley believed that the Golden Age of Constantine had been a disaster for the Church from the beginning in that it made the connection of faith with wealth and power that would continually undermine the Church's message and the nature of its summons. The end of Christendom brings to a close this unhealthy alliance. As Stuart Murray puts it:

---

19 Brown, *Religion and Society in Twentieth-Century Britain*, p. 228.

The end of Christendom marks the collapse of a determined but ultimately futile attempt to impose Christianity rather than inviting people to follow Jesus.[20]

But the problems for the Church do not end with the collapse of Christendom. Christendom-style thinking does not immediately disappear. It has been around for too long and is embedded in church structures, policies and even theological understandings, which were formed in the Christendom era. The mindset needs to be renewed and the patterning of the Church reconceived. As the title of David Clark's book has it, we need to be actively and determinedly 'breaking the mould of Christendom',[21] and this does not happen without serious reflection and work. Murray has pointed out how much work is involved in letting go of Christendom-thinking and discovering a more authentic way of being the Church after Christendom which, he argues, involves ending the disempowerment of the laity, the de-emphasizing of leadership, the reconstruction of doctrine, and ways of developing church discipline that are less connected with the power dynamics of exclusion.

This process of disengagement from Christendom-thinking and re-inventing the Church will inevitably be painful and perhaps protracted. In science fiction there is a fascination with the notion of symbiont (or symbiote) and host.[22] Symbiotic relations exist in nature. They refer to a close relationship between two organisms in which the outcome for each is highly dependent upon the other. These can be of three types: mutualism, where both organisms benefit; commensalism, where one benefits while the other is not harmed or helped; and parasitism, where one benefits but the other is harmed. SciFi extends this idea to explore moral and identity issues. In the film *Spiderman 3*, Spiderman (aka Peter Parker) is affected by an

20 Stuart Murray, *Church after Christendom*, Milton Keynes: Paternoster, 2004, p. 148.

21 Clark, *Breaking the Mould of Christendom*.

22 See, for example, the planet Trill and the creature Dax in *Star Trek: Deep Space 9*.

alien symbiote, which forms a black suit for him and enhances his powers when he wears it. However, it also brings out his darkest demons and changes Spiderman inside and out. The new powers become increasingly destructive and rob him of his better qualities until at last he decides to take off the suit (interestingly in the bell tower of a church). The struggle is hard and demanding and it is only with considerable effort and pain that the two are parted. This metaphor provides an image of the Church's alliance with power in the Christendom period from which it must now, with some effort, become free.

Issues for disciples

Again we see the issue of post-Christendom encountered in the stories of our disoriented disciples. George has lived through the period of church decline and secularization outlined by Brown. He has seen the Church lose numbers, influence and status in society and watched his own family drift from the pattern of commitment to the Church that he inherited from his parents. He has felt some of the criticisms and scandals of the Church personally and internalized a sense of marginality and impotence. He has lost confidence in his faith and carries guilt about what he sees as the failure of the Church. He hangs on to a vestige of his experience of God, for he desires to know what God wants him to do but he is lost as to how to begin. In a different way, Louise faces the reality of the Church, now exposed to public scrutiny and criticism like so many other formerly powerful institutions. She wonders whether its structures are as racist and sexist as any other organization forged in the colonial period of British history and she is considering whether her discipleship and ministry can be expressed in a church where such values have been woven into the fabric of its daily workings.

Post-Christendom poses many challenges for disciples. In the day-to-day lives of those following Jesus, decisions have constantly to be made about how to proclaim confidence in the God of our Lord Jesus Christ in the face of most people's lack of interest and cynicism about the Church's interests. We have to live as witnesses to saving grace with guilt on our hands about how the Church has misused power in the past and we have also to be engaged in dialoguing with our tradition over what of our faith is core to our identity and message and what theology was formed in Christendom that now needs to be reformed.

Conclusion: Disciples in a new world

I began the chapter by relating my sense of being lost in the city where I grew up. This city's changed landscape is analogous to the new world in which we find ourselves as disciples. It has altered almost beyond recognition over 50 years and now feels alien, uncharted and threatening to many Christians. Post-nationalism, that reconfiguring of social geography, has been built through new forms of communication and the movement and mixing up of peoples and subcultures. Post-modernity has translated some of the technological changes into cultural attitudes and values so that people are growing up with some misgivings about rationality, institutions and authority bases, with more time for emotions, and relational ways of under-standing and multi-layered, situated explanations, and with an immediate interest in experiences, images, and participation. At the same time, and due to some of the same forces, Christian-ity is moving out of its Christendom phase after a millennium and a half. Its power and influence in the state and in culture has diminished and it finds itself on the margins of mainstream society. Disciples are in the forefront of rediscovering the centre of faith and new forms of churches are forming.

In this crucible experience we disciples find that we are dis-oriented. Our identity is fragile and prone to fragmentation as we participate in many communities each with its own self understanding and way of being and each forming our identity in subtle yet powerful ways. For some disciples it is unnerving and they identify with the words of the Paul Field song 'Some-times I can't remember who I am?'.[23]

---

23 Paul Field on the album *Without a Song and Dance*, Nearfield/ICC, 2005.

Accompanying this there is *theological, ethical and moral uncertainty*. The end of Christendom means rediscovering and rebuilding how our faith relates to belief and lifestyle. Many of the old answers no longer fit, and we have less confidence in them because they were fashioned for a different world. New insights from science, art and humanities mean that we have to piece together a new collage in which faith in Jesus creates a coherent sense of all our experiences and insights. Disciples are in the vanguard of this recovery for they are having to forge Christian practices in their homes, workplaces and communities where many other perspectives exist side by side. The path is unclear and many of the old markers no longer help us. We sense that we are in a pioneering situation having to fashion fresh ways of following and new forms of church at the same time.

None of this bleak picture need be a cause of despair. As St Paul says in an equally demanding context, 'We are afflicted in every way, but not crushed; perplexed, but not driven to despair; persecuted, but not forsaken; struck down, but not destroyed' (2 Corinthians 4.9). The reason he can say this is because despite the confusing and uncharted cultural situation he finds himself in, he has a deep and life-transforming conviction, which has grown out of experience. 'For it is the God who said, "Let light shine out of darkness", who has shone in our hearts to give the light of the knowledge of the glory of God in the face of Jesus Christ' (2 Corinthians 4.6). In other words, the God of creation and the God of Jesus Christ has touched our lives and invited us to follow him, and in his face we find the glory of God. Facing the reality of the contexts of our discipleship is an important first step in taking up its challenge but the source of our life and hope is to be found in God. St Paul knows that we carry this treasure in earthen pots that can crack or break and be replaced just as the patterns of our faith and practice can be reconstructed. This is possible if we can look on God's face afresh. This is what we must do in the next chapter.

3

A Fresh Picture of God

In our house there are several pictures of the same place. It is a school that my wife's grandparents set up and ran as the main work of their adult lives and as such is important in the family's history. The school is located in attractive grounds and any one of the paintings draws the eyes into the beauty of the lawns and buildings. It looks like a nice place to visit and a good setting in which to study. But every picture is different – each painted by a different artist – and although it is not difficult to see that all the paintings are of the one place, each is distinctive and draws out features less noticed in other pictures. The eye and skill of each painter, the choice of focus and the use of light and colour allow us to appreciate some particular aspect or activity of the place.

Of course, the place changed over the 80 or so years of the school's life, with trees and bushes growing in the grounds, repair and development work carried out on the building and different seasons altering the impression too. All these factors are reflected in the paintings. What is more difficult to discern, but almost certainly at work, is the way the artists' views were shaped by the decade in which they lived and worked. Different patterns, styles and fashions in art at the time will have influenced how each artist presents the school, and with careful observation we may be able to detect some of these differences, but the issues, events and ideas of each artist's age are more hidden and involve more research and interpretation. They will nevertheless have influenced the artist in subtle ways, even on this simple landscape.

If this is true of the portrayal of a relatively uncomplicated building and its grounds, how much more is it true of the way we picture God. As we noticed in Chapter 1 on the New Testament, a fresh picture of God often emerges in response to the particular cultural setting and the issues that face Christian disciples. This fresh portrait of God is not at odds with previous images of God – it is the same God revealed in Jesus – but its freshness speaks into the contemporary dialogue between Christians and their cultural setting and helps to locate the way-markers for the path of discipleship. As in the Epistle to the Hebrews, by seeing a new image of who Christ is, the readers may find both markers of discipleship and an inspirational encouragement to take up 'the way'.

This chapter is concerned with the way we see God and involves an exploration of particular Christian ideas about God that have come to the fore in our own age. In the last chapter we attempted to identify something of the context and issues for our own time. We noted that Christian disciples today find themselves in the situation where the world has shrunk (post-national), where the long alliance between Church and state has collapsed (post-Christendom), where the culture of modernity has been profoundly questioned (post-modernity) and where people hunger for a genuine spirituality but are not inclined to look to the Church to find it. All this poses sharp theological and practical challenges for disciples that only a renewed vision of God can overcome.

In this chapter we look for a fresh picture of God for our own time and we find it in the recovery of two ideas: (1) that of the missionary God, or as it is sometimes called the *missio Dei* – the God whose love is active in the life of the world – and (2) the idea of God as a community of persons, or God the Trinity, as it is more often called. These are not fresh in the sense of new or unknown before. Rather, they represent a rediscovery and recovery of an understanding of God expressed anew in recent years by a wide range of writers. It is fair to say that many Christians have been energized and excited by these pictures of God and they are giving new impetus to the Church's understanding of itself and how it should be structured. They are also fuelling new initiatives in mission and ministry, sometimes called Fresh Expressions, new ways of being church, and there is a widespread belief that new forms of church are emerging and new patterns of ministry and mission will accompany it or perhaps bring it to birth.

However, in exploring this stimulating and life-giving vision of God, I have some worries about popular writing describing aspects of this fresh picture of God. In identifying some of the weaknesses, I want to suggest ways of speaking of God that may deepen and strengthen the picture and better equip us to be disciples of Christ for our time.

The recovery of the missionary God

Let us look first at the *missio Dei*. This term was first used in the modern period by Karl Hartenstein in 1933 but owes much to the earlier work of Karl Barth. The notion is present in several documents from Vatican II and in the latter part of the twentieth century, it was widely adopted by missiological and ecumenical theologians. It has now come to be one of the defining points of much contemporary theology.[1] The phrase is a Latin term which is usually translated as 'mission of God' or 'sending of God' and it has sometimes been taken to refer to God's sending of Jesus into the world. It is better understood, however, as referring to the missionary character of God – the way God always is – which is expressed in the incarnation, the sending of the Spirit and other acts of God.

Anyone who has not met this term before may be surprised by it. Many people outside the Church encounter the word mission in the form of mission statements, written to express what a company or business exists for and with which employees

---

1 The thinking and writing about the *missio Dei* is recounted in various places. See, for example, David J. Bosch, *Transforming Mission: Paradigm Shifts in Theology of Mission*, New York: Orbis, 1991. Andrew Kirk, *What is Mission?* London: Darton, Longman & Todd, 1999. Paul Avis, *A Ministry Shaped by Mission*, London and New York: T&T Clark, 2005, pp. 4ff.

need to become familiar so that they can work with the purpose of the company. Such a person might well ask: 'What! Does God have mission or purpose?' and the answer would be a profound 'Yes!' God's mission can be described as loving the world. The world and all its creatures are the object of God's love and it is this loving that is the source and direction of God's action. As John 3.16 puts it, 'God so loved the world that . . .' In other words, God's attitude towards the world is one of profound and unfathomable care and concern, which continually issues in action. The overarching story of the Bible, sometimes called the meta-narrative, is about God reaching out in love. Love gives birth to the created order, love issues in the rich and seemingly inexhaustible abundance and variety of life to arise on the earth, love nurtures the possibilities of consciousness, fosters creatures with free will and their own creative power and, even when free will and human power results in damage and destruction, love seeks to heal, remake and renew creation.

Here is a working definition of the *missio Dei*: 'God's loving activity in creating, sustaining and redeeming the world'. In this brief and inevitably inadequate statement there are some points to note:

1 It is *God's* activity

Mission, as many people have pointed out, has often been thought of as something the Church does or that particular people are sent to do in or for the Church. In the nineteenth century and the early twentieth century mission was what Christian missionaries did in going oversees to spread the gospel. When I was a young Christian of 16 years of age I was part of what was called a 'Young People's Mission Band' which went around churches singing, giving testimonies and leading services. Theological and Bible colleges often assemble and send out mission teams for faith-sharing weekends or to help with particular church tasks. All these are appropriate uses of the word 'mission', for the root meaning of '*missio*' is sending, and each of these different groups is sent. Our definition, however, helps us to see that, in theological terms, the primary sending or mission is that of God. It is God who sends and God who is sent. If the Church or people in the Church are sent, this is derivative activity. That is, it is dependent on, initiated and empowered by the mission of God. God is the activist to be found at the heart of what is happening in the world. The Christian calling is, at its core, learning what God is doing and joining in. In some ways, new employees being shown the mission statement of the company and being asked to become familiar with it, perhaps even to learn it by heart, is a good analogy. Christian disciples are people who become familiar with the character and purpose of God, who trust that God is working in the world and join in. God is, however, the prime mover, the first and defining missionary and thus the locus of all missionary activity. In other words, in a Christian framework, mission is understood as being derived from the very nature of God.

2　It is God's activity *now*

The definition is in the present tense. It is not what God did in the past, at the beginning of the world, in ancient history or even in the life and death and resurrection of Jesus. The *missio Dei* is concerned with the work of God in the world now, God's continuing being and work in the present. This is not saying that God and the world are the same thing, nor that everything that is happening in the world is God's activity. God has made space for autonomy and contingency in creation and for the actions of free-willed beings. But God is not absent from the world either. Some people speak of the *missio Dei* as the sphere of God in the midst of the world. As we noticed earlier, central to Jesus' message was the notion of the kingdom or rule of God, the divine reality close to people in their everyday reality, always ready to break in to challenge, heal, restore and renew. In Jesus' teaching the completion or fulfilment of the kingdom of God is in the future, but he also emphasized the present reality of God's activity. As we will see later, it is the kingdom of God as seen in the life and teaching of Jesus that is a key reference point for discerning the work of God in the world, but we emphasize at this point the crucial importance of God's activity here and now.

3 It is God's activity now *in and for the world*

We need to be clear that the object of God's love and activity is not in the first instance the Church but the world. It is the world that God so loves, according to our text, 'that he sent his Son' and it is the world that Christ died to save. And it is the world, according to the Book of Revelation, that will be made new at the fulfilment of God's purposes. Thus, we are to find God in the life of the world. This is important when we consider the Church. Just as it is not the Church's mission but God's mission that is first, so God's love for and action in the world need to be kept in mind in order for the Church to find its orientation. It is in the world that we must look for the signs and signals of God. Thus, the life and work of God will not only be found in the Church. The Church has a special place and purpose in the mission of God, in receiving the life-transforming good news of God's love and seeking to live out in word and deed the reality of God's kingdom. The Church is to share in God's mission and to pass on to all creation the good news. As Martyn Atkins puts it, the people of God are 'the product of God's mission, and then participants and partners in God's mission'.[2] The world, with its human family, however, remains the focus of God's loving and also the place of finding God. How the Church is organized and what forms it takes should be determined by our commitment to the mission of God or, to put it in more theological language, our ecclesiology is a function of our missiology.

God the Trinity

In some respects, the exploration of God as Trinity might be seen to be a separate piece of theology and concerned with

2 Martyn Atkins, *Resourcing Renewal: Shaping Churches for the Emerging Future,* Peterborough: Inspire, 2007, p. 12.

very different interests. For those who study the writing of the early Church it is obvious that many words were devoted to this subject, seemingly to solve a very tricky problem: namely how to speak with coherence of God as one and yet three. In some ways the New Testament, which doesn't use the word Trinity, creates rather than solves the problem by affirming the monotheism of its Jewish roots (Mark 12.29–30) and at the same time speaking of God as Father, Son and Spirit.[3] It would be possible to conclude that the doctrine of the Trinity is an attempt to solve a paradox for the sake of rational thinking people becoming Christian disciples. Solving this paradox is no easy task as many can testify. No wonder that St Augustine said 'anyone who denies the Trinity is in danger of losing salvation, but anyone who tries to understand it is in danger of losing his mind'.[4]

The truth is, of course, more subtle and more relevant for us in our time. Naturally, in revisiting the doctrine of the Trinity scholars have been concerned for coherence in order to be able to give a reasonable account of the faith (1 Peter 3.15), but their revisiting has also opened up some exciting insights into what Trinity means for human flourishing, the nature of the Church and the mission of God. Much has been made of what is called the 'Social Trinity' and the way that this has been understood is through a Greek word 'perichoresis'. This term, used by a group called the Cappadocian Fathers,[5] conveys a sense of mutually

---

3 References to the Spirit and Son as divine are scattered through the New Testament. See particularly John's Gospel. Matthew 28 indicates baptism is to be in the name of the Father, Son and Spirit. Ephesians 4.4–7 manages to affirm one God and yet speaks of the Spirit and Christ as part of the confession of faith.

4 Roger E. Olson and Christopher A. Hall, *The Trinity*, Grand Rapids: Eerdmans, 2002, p. 1.

5 Basil, Gregory of Nyssa and Gregory Naziansus. For a discussion of the term 'perichoresis' see Jürgen Moltmann, *The Trinity and the Kingdom of God*, London: SCM Press, 1981; John D. Zizioulas, *Being as Communion*, New York: St Vladimir's Seminary Press, 1985 and Colin Gunton, *The One, The Three and the Many*, Cambridge: Cambridge University Press, 1993.

indwelling persons who are distinct and yet wholly interdependent, persons so sensitive and attuned to each other that they are as one, they know as one, will as one and act as one. An image that is sometimes used to illustrate the idea is that of a beautiful dance where the co-ordination is flawless and where the dancers are so in tune with each other in the performance of the dance that you might think there is actually only one dancer. This image fits well with St Augustine's notion of the Trinity as like the mind, made up of memory, understanding and will, in that all three are involved in the exercise of any one aspect. But by shifting the metaphors towards a community of persons, however, another set of imaginative connections is made. So it is possible to say that community is at the heart of God and that in God's love for the world the divine community is opened to embrace the created order and its human persons. In other words, to respond to God is to take up the invitation to participate in the community of God.

The use of the term 'person' is not accidental or incidental here, for this social understanding of the Trinity resonates with much that we have learned of how people grow into their particular and unique characters. Social psychologists argue that we are formed as persons in and through our relationships and that our concept of self grows out of the communities to which we belong and in which we participate.

You may have had the experience of working in a good team. I have had experience of good and bad team work. In the very best experiences something exciting happens. You get a buzz from being with the other members, you look forward to working with them, you feel valued and wanted and energetic and you have confidence in the task you are undertaking. In such a team there are amazing effects: you feel safe and supported and so are prepared to take risks; the love and support in one brings out the gifts in another; your weaknesses and faults are known but are not a source of shame nor do they inhibit the work of the team – rather, people in the team work in such a way that their various strengths are put to work for others; and you sense that the whole is greater than the sum of the parts, that more was made possible through the team relationships than might have been achieved by the individuals' contributions separately made. Perhaps most importantly, the experience has profound and permanent effects on who you are. Through the team you grow in your person and sense of self. This is one example of person being formed in relationship. Being in community, therefore, should not diminish our personality but enable us to grow towards our full selves. In relation to thinking about God, our good team experience is a very human analogy to the Trinity but it is suggestive of another thought. The invitation to share in the life of God, the divine community, is an invitation to be formed in relationship to God and so discover and realize our true selves. Robin Greenwood notes that the qualities associated with the notion of *perichoresis* are exactly those that promise a more fulfilled humanity: mutuality, face-to-face reciprocity, being in openness, communion of difference. These are the advanced signs of human society free of injustice and oppression and as such are taken up enthusiastically by the liberation theologian Leonardo Boff.[6]

Finally, Social Trinitarianism locates the origin and sources of mission (the *missio Dei*) as the heart of God and in the continual movement between the persons of the Trinity. John's Gospel captures this in profound images and words. It is the Father who sends the Son into the world (John 3.16), the Son who returns to the Father (John 13.1), the Spirit who is sent by the Father at the request of the Son (John 14.26) to be alongside the disciples to lead into truth (John 16.13) and bring new birth (John 3.8). The sending of the disciples (John 21.21–3) is in the context of this dynamic movement within God and is accompanied by the sending of the Spirit (21.23), a sign, symbol and empowering seal of the missionary God. In other words, to link up with our previous comments on the *missio Dei*, the movement of sending begins in the heart of God. Mission stems from the dynamic interplay of the Trinity, and this divine com-

---

6 Quoted in Robin Greenwood, *Transforming Church: Liberating Structures for Ministry*, London: SPCK, 2002, p. 83.

munity of persons in loving and transforming movement is to be found in the world.

Oddly, the notion of paradox becomes in this rediscovery not so much a problem to be solved but a better way of seeing deeper truth. Just as we now know that understanding such things as quantum physics requires more than one way of seeing the same thing, so some truths are only approachable by paradox. It is in their seeming contradiction that we glimpse their depth and exciting reality.

The picture of God to emerge from these twin themes of Trinity and *missio Dei* is exhilarating and in many ways liberating for the Church and Christian disciples at the beginning of the twenty-first century, for it speaks to our particular situation and issues. In a post-modern age where individualism is a driving force and people seek self-fulfilment and personal realization through experience and relationship, the God made known to us in Christ is one who invites us to find our true self in relationship with the divine community, wherein we are formed into the unique and special persons that we are called to be in and through relationship. In a context where Christendom has collapsed and where the Church finds itself unsure of how to be church, how to unlearn some of its inherited patterns and theology, how to live faithfully in a world where it is marginalized and sometimes despised, God is again seen as an outgoing God who calls us to follow into mission and partnership in God's work. We are thus to seek to discern the Spirit working in the world and experiment with new ways of being church. In a situation where many people are hungry and thirsty for the spiritual dimension to life but where religion is seen as the opposite of spirituality, we Christians are to celebrate the *missio Dei* which 'speaks of the overflowing of the love of God's being and nature into the purposeful activity of the world'.[7] We can invite people to make connections between their already developed sense of God and the Christian story. And in a world in which social geography has been radically reconfigured, bringing us ever closer to one another and the

---

7 Avis, *A Ministry Shaped by Mission*, p. 5.

variety of cultures and faiths on the planet, we find a God who crosses over, surmounting the most obstinate and resistant of barriers to reach out to her children, inviting us to join in the same type of outgoing, boundary-crossing enterprise.

Signs of new life

Some of the renewal that this fresh picture of God promises is already underway. In 2004 the Church of England published *Mission-shaped Church* (MSC) which set out an agenda for the new developments in patterns of church life, church planting and fresh expressions of church. Its theological section[8] draws on some of the thinking about God as Trinity and the *missio Dei,* which we have identified above, and extends these in the direction of ecclesiology through discussion about incarnation and the notion of inculturation. The implications are clear that a church trusting in a missionary Trinitarian God as revealed in Jesus will face the prospect of massive cultural and societal change confidently, prepared to let go of much that has been precious and take risks in starting and forming churches for the future. Since then, a series of initiatives and a raft of books have followed.[9]

In September 2004 the Church of England and the Methodist Church, building on their shared Covenant, launched a five-year project entitled 'Fresh Expressions' with the specific aim 'to resource mission through encouraging new and different expressions of church life'. Fresh Expressions are by definition diverse and varied and include initiatives such as alternative worship gatherings, café churches, cell churches, youth con-

8 *Mission-shaped Church: Church Planting and Fresh Expressions of Church in a Changing Context*, London: Church House Publishing, 2005, pp. 84–103.

9 See Margaret Withers, *Mission-shaped Children*, London: Church House Publishing, 2006; Paul Bayes and Tim Sledge, *Mission-shaped Parish*, London: Church House Publishing, 2006; Susan Hope, *Mission-shaped Spirituality: The Transforming Power of Mission*, London: Church House Publishing, 2007; Sally Gaze, *Mission-shaped and Rural*, London: Church House Publishing, 2007.

gregations and network-focused Christian communities. Some represent simply the change of style within an inherited church context, others are new ventures in non-traditional venues, while yet others take the shape of new networks and new ways of relating Christians together. One forms its life around a twice per week bread-baking event and another offers a safe and holy space for late-night clubbers. There is a Goth community at Coventry Cathedral and an initiative to work with the migratory surfers who travel the coastal beaches in search of the great waves. At the end of 2007 the Fresh Expression Directory listed over 600 registered fresh expressions in the UK.[10]

Alongside the initiatives in church life, much time is being given to thinking about ministry in and beyond the life of the gathered Church. Greenwood has used the theological base of *missio Dei* and Trinity to argue for the development of local ministries as a major way of accompanying and developing significant change in the life of the church. David Clark and Paul Avis both make a claim that diaconal ministry should now be recovered with a new focus and identity in the light of the rediscovery of the missionary God. Building on the work done by Collins,[11] which argues that deacons were not and should not be seen as models of servanthood with the emphasis on lowly practical work (the modern equivalent of distributing food or washing feet) but as missionary ministers, proclaiming the gospel through translation into particular cultures and languages, Avis wants the rhetoric of humble service to be dropped[12] and instead for the diaconate to be understood in terms of a sign of the Church's mission as deacons relate to the needs of the unchurched in the community. Clark wants to go further, seeing deacons as the focus and reminder of the calling

---

10 A visit to the Fresh Expression Directory on 30 November 2007 found 402 Anglican, 155 Methodist, 33 Ecumenical and 10 Baptist registered FX initiatives, with a handful from other denominations.

11 J. N. Collins, *Diakonia: Re-Interpreting the Ancient Sources*, Oxford: Oxford University Press, 1990.

12 Avis, *A Ministry Shaped by Mission*, p. 110–11.

of the church for dispersed church – lay people in their daily lives.[13] Deacons should be primarily community educators, facilitating theological reflection on daily life and work. The churches, in the light of the commitment to *Fresh Expressions*, have embarked on new thinking about the training and deployment of pioneer ministers, lay and ordained, and are working on implementing patterns of selection, training, authorization and deployment. In addition, there is much talk of pioneer ministries – lay and ordained – which will forge new types of community and patterns of relationships. All this resonates deeply with the picture of God as missionary and community creating.

Yet another interesting area of development has been attention to Christians in the workplace in the light of this view about God. For many industrial chaplains, activists and writers, the workplace needs now to be recognized as a mission field, a place where the missionary God is already labouring. The website of *Transform Work UK*[14] is dedicated to supporting Christians in the workplace as they seek to 'work in a godly way; to reach out to their colleagues with the good news of Jesus Christ; to live out their faith in the context of professional or workplace Christian groups; to cope with the difficulties and stresses associated with the UK workplace; to be salt and light in their immediate environments; and make a difference wherever God has placed them'. Some have seen this revisiting of the idea of God at work quite narrowly in terms of the workplace primarily as a location for evangelism through work-based friendship.[15] Other writers attempt to build a broader understanding of work as a way of sharing in the creative processes of God[16] and

---

13 David Clark, *Breaking the Mould of Christendom: Kingdom Community, Diaconal Church and the Liberation of the Laity*, Peterborough: Epworth, 2005.

14 http://www.transformworkuk.org/

15 G. Shattock, *Wake up to Work*, Bletchley: Scripture Union, 1999; M. Greene, *Thank God It's Monday*, Bletchley: Scripture Union, 1994.

16 See, for example, Ken Costa, *God at Work*, London and New York: Continuum, 2007.

examining work through theological eyes.[17] Again this is not a new area of interest. Industrial chaplaincy has been going since the 1940s, French worker priests were active between 1942 and 1954, and the Faith and Life movement, which began in 1925, was one of the streams that formed the World Council of Churches. What is new is the reconnecting of the *missio Dei* and the Trinitarian God with the world of work.

This fresh image of God has also enabled a new kind of Christian identity to arise which allows Christians from formerly very different convictions and emphases to find common cause. Those who would have put weight on Christian conversion and evangelism now embrace social action not as an optional outworking of faith but as fundamental to mission. Likewise, those who might have centred their Christian identity in serving others and engaging with the struggles for justice in the world, now own that witnessing to faith and inviting others to follow Christ is essential also. Those on every side who found it difficult to live with diversity and difference recognize that a community of persons in mission carries at its heart variety and multiplicity and is stronger for it. This new Christian identity might be called an open or liberal evangelicalism.

The evangelicalism that inhabits the new world of Fresh Expressions and emerging church is attractive, amenable, human, and indeed exciting. It can live with different ways of reading the scriptures, it puts human relationships at the heart of evangelism, it uses common sense in its decision making, it is prepared to relegate to a lower order issues which were formerly identity defining and it no longer wants to control the outcomes of witness into clone-like patterns of church (even inherited evangelical ones). It lives with post-modernity in a surprisingly creative way. On the one hand, it accepts easily that people are shaped by post-modernity on a day-to-day level and therefore can affirm them and get alongside them in this culture, and it takes delight in the diversity (and the diversity

---

17 See Andrew Stokes, *Working with God: Faith and Life at Work*, Ethics: Our Choices series, ed. Stephen Platten, London and New York: Mowbray, 1992.

valuing nature) of this contemporary culture which creates the fertile soil for Fresh Expressions. At the same time, it lives by the meta-narrative of God's loving, redeeming action in the world and continues to be critical of consumerist ideology and practice. The reconnection of mission and evangelism with the resulting breadth in the latter and bite in the former is also to be welcomed. We have the beginnings of a renewed theology and practice in the life of the Church that can be owned widely and engaged with energetically, and we are indebted to those who have patiently worked through significant issues and helped us rediscover purpose and direction.

But it is exactly in the energy and enthusiasm that is now flowing that we risk losing the richness of the new-found picture of God. Despite all the excitement around the refreshed picture of God, I feel uncomfortable with some of the literature on Mission-shaped Church, Fresh Expressions and Faith and Work and detect real dangers.

Some failings in our current view of God

The moments of disquiet arise when the missiological major key of the symphony suggests that there is very little of worth in the world. It comes in slightly subtle but telling language patterns. For example, there are many authors in the collection of essays that make up *Let My People Grow*[18] who urge whole-life discipleship – disciples who live integrated transformative lives that affect the world around. At first sight this is very attractive. I find myself agreeing whole-heartedly that the workplace of many Christians has been neglected as a place of lived discipleship and ministry; that people have compartmentalized their lives; that the barrier of sacred and secular is an artificial one; and that churches are often unsuccessful in nurturing discipleship because they do not take this major sphere of most Christians' lives seriously. As Steve Davie puts it:

18 Mark Greene and Tracy Cotterell (eds), *Let My People Grow: Making Disciples Who Make a Difference in Today's World*, Milton Keynes: Authentic Media, 2006.

churches have a tendency to lock in to the local neighbour-
hood and pay little attention to the places where their members are living and working throughout the week. And the
church often presents spiritual growth as somehow divorced
from life in the real world. These limited perspectives shape
our approach to disciple-making.[19]

All agree that Christians should be better equipped for and supported in their work lives. Look further, however, and you find
only one-way traffic. Christians are agents of transformation in
their workplace, they are there to shape the context according
to Christian values and to demonstrate holy living.[20] The language is all about what Christians take to, and do in their places
of work. The workplace is thus subtly portrayed as a godless
territory to be regained for Christ. There isn't much emphasis
on learning from God, who may be in the workplace, being
challenged by the kindness and generosity of a non-Christian,
delighting in the creativity, insight and beauty that work can
produce. Where is the opportunity for Christian workers to
reflect on what they have discovered in their work experience
together, to bring home to the gathered Church the joy, not
just of seeing a person becoming a Christian or a hard-won
value being firmly embedded in an employer's policy – these are
indeed great sources of joy – but of encountering genuine godly
devotion in a Hindu colleague, forgiveness in business practice
or the buzz of creativity in completing a team task? These too
may be witnesses to God's presence and action. Christians have
no monopoly on these activities, though they may be called to
identify, celebrate and give thanks for all glimpses of God.

Another example of one-way traffic is evident in the kind of
spirituality being advocated for MSC. Susan Hope's book[21] is
very stimulating and conveys strongly the idea that the spirit-

---

19 Steve Davie, 'Why Do Churches Resist Disciple-Making', in
Greene and Cotterell (eds) *Let My People Grow*.

20 Lawrence Singlehurst, 'Lessons from Cell', in Greene and Cotterell
(eds) *Let My People Grow*.

21 Hope, *Mission-shaped Spirituality*.

uality needed is one that echoes the missionary enterprise and enables communities and individuals to sustain their apostolic calling. Her chapter on 'seeing' is brimming with evocative ideas. She portrays a 'seeing' spirituality as a kind of *'contemplation, seeing deeply, seeing into the heart of things,'*[22] such as Jesus displayed when he saw the crowds (or the leper or outcast) and was moved in love to respond. Components of this 'seeing' are threefold: **Awareness** – to see the reality of people and situations, **intentionality** – to identify particular groups or individuals and a desire to discern a response, and **imagination** to see creative possibilities for response. With these features of 'seeing' one can act like Jesus, who 'manages to be deeply moved by what he encounters in the suffering of others without being so overwhelmed that he cannot see God's creative possibilities in the given moment'.[23] This is a valuable insight for a mission-oriented Church to engage with the struggles and suffering of those around them. But surely there is another dimension to 'seeing', one that recognizes the signs of the kingdom in unlikely places, such as the Syro-Phoenician woman, the centurion and a compassionate Samaritan. The same might be claimed for the parables of the kingdom, some of which must have grown out of Jesus' observation of the world around him: extravagant seed-sowers, diligent shepherds and generous banquet givers. These too point to the character of God. While there is much to be healed, restored and forgiven, there is also much to delight in and be amazed by – all pointing to the presence and activity of God in the world. Hope, like so many other writers in the field, implies that Christian spirituality is about what the Church can bring to others, and not so much about what might be received.

John Hull's theological critique of the *Mission-shaped Church*[24] identifies a similar concern in the text of the original publication. He accuses the writers of imperialism in their disregard of the reality and the diversity of other faiths. The

---

22 Hope, *Mission-shaped Spirituality*, p. 23.

23 Hope, *Mission-shaped Spirituality*, p. 22.

24 John M. Hull, *Mission-shaped Church: A Theological Response*, London: SCM Press, 2006.

imagery of growth and reproduction used in the theological section of *Mission-shaped Church*,[25] viewing the Church as the heir of promise to Abraham with a 'divine mandate to reproduce' and to 'fill the earth', leaves no standing room for Jews and Muslims, despite the fact that they see themselves also as Abraham's children. Indeed, the lack of recognition of other faiths in general is noticeable by its absence. Where they are noted, other cultures and faiths are generally seen negatively, as reinforcing consumerism and as competitors and nowhere acknowledged as enriching British society.

Perhaps most penetrating is Hull's concern that the discussion of inculturation in *Mission-shaped Church* is selective, encouraging the Church to take seriously the context of consumerism and thus becoming better shaped for mission but keeping the discussion firmly focused on structures for mission, rather than anything more demanding. For Hull, at the heart of inculturation studies there is an openness to the discovery of (something of) the gospel within culture, which may in turn cause us to re-assess our own understanding or even surrender some theological conceptualizations for the sake of a larger, more comprehensive, knowledge. He does not see this in *Mission-shaped Church*.

> There is no trace in *Mission-shaped Church* of the methodology of seeking in the surrounding culture for the rumour of angels or signals of transcendence.[26]

Hull commends the section in *Mission-shaped Church* on the notion of the '*spermatikos*' (Christ's presence in all cultures) advocated by Justin Martyr, but complains that it is not applied to other faith communities or cultures. The Church is called on to adapt and sacrifice for the missionary task but the adaptation and sacrifice are always to do with structures, not to do with concepts or theology or the nature of faith itself. He believes

---

25 *Mission-shaped Church: Church Planting and Fresh Expressions of Church in a Changing Context*, pp. 80–103.
26 Hull, *Mission-shaped Church*, p. 26.

that this reveals a 'denial of the presence of the gospel in the receiving culture prior to the arrival of the Christian faith'.

Again this is one-way traffic. The Church is the agent and the world the recipient. Rather than the Church moving to join the missionary God who is at work in the world in many and various ways already, the Church is the normative, if not the sole, agent of God's mission.

Hull contends that the problem arises because mission is seen through the lens of the Church and not the Church through the lens of mission, as is claimed by *Mission-shaped Church*. Had it been thoroughly missiological, then the Church would not be seen as an object of mission. Rather the Church would have been seen as a mission project, part of the wider initiative of God in the world he loves. *Mission-shaped Church* was, he argues, an attempt to help parish churches stuck in decline find new ways of responding to their calling, but the larger missiological framework employed has been badly handled and ended up being too heavily church focused.

Whether or not Hull is right and fair on the writers of *Mission-shaped Church*, there is sufficient evidence, I think, to see a recurring undercurrent in the language and metaphors running through much of the literature. This reveals a view of the Church in its missionary endeavours as always being the carrier of Christ, bringing him to the world and rarely, if ever, being a recipient from God in any place other than the gathered Church and from any sources other than the ecclesial community. The story of Cornelius (Acts 9—10), now much beloved of *missio Dei* advocates, is a genuine two-way exchange resulting in the greater enrichment of the experience of God for both Peter and Cornelius, but this seems not to be genuinely expected or anticipated in much of the popular writing on this topic. It is rare to find this sentiment in any of the accompanying stories in the *Mission-shaped Church* series.

Martyn Atkins makes a strong case for the Church attending to its own language.[27] He is concerned with the body language

---

27 Atkins, *Resourcing Renewal: Shaping Churches for the Emerging Future*.

of the local church and how others read it, often very differently from us. The kind of self-aware listening he encourages would serve us well here. For the indicative 'language patterns, voice, movement, breathing, and posture' of the literature cited convey a singular view of the Church as holding the answers with nothing much to receive or learn, except how to get alongside people in contemporary culture. It may not be intended, indeed I think it is not, but you don't have to be an expert in discourse analysis to get the picture that underpins these writings.

We need to correct this picture primarily because it is not faithful to the core notion of *missio Dei*. The great missiologist, David Bosch, writes that God's turning to the world in respect of creation, care, redemption and consummation 'takes place in ordinary human history, not exclusively in and through the church'[28] and warns us against claiming too much for ourselves: 'The church. . . has no monopoly on God's reign, may not claim it for itself, may not present itself as the realized kingdom of God over against the world.'[29] The Church is called by God into mission to receive from God at work in the world as well as sharing its testimony and this needs to be reflected in the popular language of *Mission-shaped church* and Fresh Expressions and in the 'success' stories that are told.

Dangers

There are real dangers if we do not attend to this. Let me name some of them:

1   We fail to catch glimpses of God

It is possible to walk down a street many hundreds of times and not notice the beautiful architecture higher on the buildings than our eyes tend to look. It is possible to come across a word or idea or sport that you have never noticed before, but discover it is very familiar to other members of your family or friends.

---

28 Bosch, *Transforming Mission*, p. 391.
29 Bosch, *Transforming Mission*, p. 517.

In both cases we simply have not noticed. Much of what we notice is determined by the way we have come to see things and the expectations that accompany our world view (or cognitive structure as psychologists sometime describe it).[30] In effect, our world view filters what we encounter so we attend to things that are familiar and expected. In a similar way, a consequence of our current language about mission may be that we assume that there is nothing of God to find away from the gathered Church and, like the disciples on the Emmaus road, miss recognizing Jesus who is alongside us. Indeed, we may be so busy witnessing and seeking to change our community, workplace and family that we think 'no good thing' can come from 'those places' and fail to see the very One we want to serve. Part of the role of Christian education in the gathered Church is to train our seeing, by making us familiar with the character of God in scripture and tradition, so that we can discern him in the midst of life. Without a more robust notion of the *missio Dei* in our churches we will preach and teach a view of God that skews people's perception and response to God only in terms of that which is saved from the world or conquered within it. Without a view of God as meeting us in the midst of the life of the world we will not notice the Spirit at work in these places and we will not tell each other the stories of surprising grace and goodness. I long to find the modern-day equivalent of John V. Taylor's suggestion that the curved bar, which by its design encourages people to talk to each other, may have been the working of the Spirit.[31]

2 We fail to nurture appropriate praise and thanksgiving

It is not uncommon for people to complain about the disappearance of basic manners. 'People don't say please and thank you', is a regular refrain. Whether our society is worse

---

30 See Jennifer A. Moon, *Reflection in Learning and Professional Development*, London: Kogan Page, 1999.

31 John V. Taylor, *The Go-between God: The Holy Spirit and the Christian Mission*, first American ed., Philadelphia: Fortress Press, 1973, p. 40.

than any previous one I am not sure, but it is true that people will not say 'thank you' for things that they have not noticed. Thus, people who fail to catch some surprising and gracious glimpses of God will not give thanks for these and the worship of the gathered Church will be deprived of these joys and delights in God.

Worship is, of course, more than praise and thanksgiving but without these elements it would be hard to sketch out a notion of what worship is. In worship we turn to face the God who loves us and has shown himself to us. We declare (in word and action) God's great acts, confess our sins, offer our thanksgiving and open ourselves and the world to God's purposes. We praise God for his extraordinary character and thank God for her goodness. In our encounter with God we acknowledge God's transforming love, and often find ourselves caught up in it.

It is possible to argue that worship is part of the *missio Dei*. This is the case made by Paul Avis,[32] where the core functions of the Church – preaching and teaching, celebrating the sacraments and pastoral care – constitute the mission of the Church without remainder.[33] However, apart from the slightly uncomfortable logical difficulty implicit in this assertion that the mission of God is to create the worship of God, it may be better to conceive of worship, at least in part, in terms of our human response to the extraordinary graciousness, goodness and love of God. In this sense, the nurture of praise and thankfulness in the people of God will be in response to proclamation and encounter with God in worship and the joyous gathering of people who have also discovered this to be true in the midst of God's world. Glimpsing God and taking time to offer our thanks and telling the stories to each other may capture what Alan Ecclestone called 'making the most of our moments of perception'.[34] This we will not be able to do if we

---

32 Avis, *A Ministry Shaped by Mission.*

33 Avis, *A Ministry Shaped by Mission*, pp. 20–1.

34 Alan Ecclestone, *Yes to God*, London: Darton, Longman & Todd, 1984.

confine God's activity to the Church and assume that we must carry it to the world.

3 Our servanthood is 'sloping'

Atkins helpfully points out that how we go about mission and service carries many subliminal messages. Thus, much of nineteenth-century mission of the church (overseas and in Britain) conveyed the assumption of superiority – 'us down to them' attitude – whether that was in care for the poor in our cities or schools or for the developing nation. This approach of superiority he calls 'Sloping'. It continues in many forms now.[35] Thus, he argues that in order to engage with contemporary society which is (rightly) suspicious of 'sloping' we need to move to another form of servanthood that is not sloping, but much more on a level, supporting and serving people as friends and neighbours in their projects and interests and needs – quoting John Robinson he suggests that this is being a servant in someone else's house.[36] In order to do this, however, we have to believe that people's interests and needs are important in their own right and can be affirmed and encouraged. An instrumentalist view would be seen for what it is. We can only take part in such serving if we can delight in others' lives and activities and are open to receive from them. Thus, a view of *missio Dei* that sees the world as without goodness and offers only a one-way flow from Christians to others will inevitably convey a sloping service.

4 Our view of the world becomes dualistic

A one-way understanding of the Church's involvement in mission will be Gnostic in flavour. Only those things we have discovered from the revelation in Jesus Christ will be counted as worthwhile and all else deemed worthless unless redeemed by contact with that message which we are carrying. Just as

---

35 Atkins, *Resourcing Renewal*. See his comments on the images underlying much of our recent work: e.g. landlord/tenant, teacher/pupil and therapist/patient, p. 126.

36 Atkins, *Resourcing Renewal*, p. 124.

Irenaeus had to resist the Gnostic idea that the material world was evil, the creation of a lesser God, so we must avoid popular (mis)understandings of the mission of God, which denigrate the world around us and its people. Ironically, in our desire to get alongside post-modern culture (which Leonard Sweet refers to as 'kissing' the culture[37]) we have allowed the missionary discourse to become implicitly dualistic, unwilling to seek the traces of God in creation, unready to receive the scattering of divine gifts and unprepared to behold God's immanent presence. One of the key criticisms of the Radical Orthodoxy group and much of the post-liberalism in general is that it traps Christian theology and the Church into a separate sphere, cut off from the world and other discourses.[38] This is a travesty of the creation as made by God. It also sits uncomfortably with the doctrine of incarnation and ultimately condemns theology to talk only to itself.

Against these dangers, we must, I think, look for ways of continuing with the missionary zeal we are experiencing and at the same time develop a more balanced concept of the *missio Dei*.

The missionary God who meets us

Another stream of writing appearing alongside the Fresh Expressions and emerging church discourse, and sometimes not so noticed, is the emphasis on learning of God from the ordinary. Jeff Astley's flagship book *Ordinary Theology*[39] signalled the beginning of a new area of research and reflection concentrating not on the theology articulated by professionals (academics or clergy) but as held by ordinary Christians. It concerns itself with what ordinary Christians believe and how that belief is

---

37 Leonard Sweet, *Post-Modern Pilgrims*, Nashville: BH Publishing, 2000.

38 Steven Shakespeare, *Radical Orthodoxy: A Critical Introduction*, London: SPCK, 2007.

39 Jeff Astley, *Ordinary Theology*, Explorations in Practical, Pastoral and Empirical Theology, ed. Leslie J. Francis and Jeff Astley, Aldershot: Ashgate, 2002.

shaped and lived. In the process of painstaking investigation through careful interviews and observation it exposes gaps between 'orthodox' accounts and lived reality. These might call for correction, helping people find a more robust faith, but equally the gaps might be sources of challenge to the tradition, causing us to revisit and reshape particular ideas formed in the past that are no longer able to provide confidence on which to base lived Christian faith.[40] Some emerging church writers recognize this too. Stuart Murray, for example, sees emerging church as currently being prepared to be more culturally creative than theologically innovative. He suggests that one of the challenges of post-Christendom is to take more theological risks and be prepared to revisit theological ideas that were forged in Christendom and which no longer communicate vibrant good news.[41] What is significant here is the expectation that there is something of God to be learned from the seemingly ordinary and mundane, which might reform theology.

In addressing New Spirituality John Drane develops a similar line.[42] His research into the widespread and growing interest in spirituality leads him to the conclusion that spirituality is embedded in human physiology. In addition to the work of Alistair Hardy and more recently David Hay, who have chronicled many accounts of spiritual experience among children and adults with no religious background, Drane cites recent work of geneticists, chemists and neuroscientists finding evidence of links between the body/brain, even DNA, and 'spiritual' experiences.[43] If this is true, then spirituality may be hardwired in

---

40 See Jeff Astley and Ann Christie, *Taking Ordinary Theology Seriously*, Cambridge: Grove, 2007.

41 Stuart Murray, *Church after Christendom*, Milton Keynes: Paternoster, 2004.

42 John Drane, *Do Christians Know How to Be Spiritual?*, London: Darton, Longman & Todd, 2005.

43 See Dean H. Hamer, *God Gene: How Faith Is Hardwired into Our Genes*, New York and London: Doubleday, 2004. Rick Strassman, *Dmt: The Spirit Molecule: A Doctor's Revolutionary Research into the Biology of Near-Death and Mystical Experiences*, Rochester, VT: Park Street Press, 2000. Andrew B. Newberg, Eugene G. D'Aquili and Vince

human beings and the search for experience of God beyond the Church is unsurprising in a post-religious age. Drane speaks of spirituality as 'the software of humankind'[44] capable of many forms and continually seeking to make contact with God. He worries, however, that the Church is afraid of this new spirituality and tends to demonize rather than trying to understand this 'secular' mysticism. He advocates an approach to mission, modelled on Paul in Athens (Acts 17), which listens before speaking, is prepared to journey with people and which does not carry unrealistic expectations. The underlying conviction is that people may already be in touch with the reality of God in the world before they hear the Christian message. This is to be acknowledged and delighted in, even if added to, developed, challenged and re-channelled.

Clive Marsh's book *Christ in Practice: A Christology of Everyday Life*[45] goes a stage further. This book, the second in a two-part project, is a serious academic argument, seeking to extend and supplement the ideas of Dietrich Bonhoeffer on Christology. Bonhoeffer's haunting question, 'Who is Christ for us today?', raises the associated question of where to find Christ today. Answering his own questions, the famous German theologian martyr spoke of Christ experienced in community, though for him this meant the gathered Church and, given his situation, it meant the true Christian community in which Christ is present in word and sacrament. Marsh wants to extend this idea of Christ as present in community and speaks of ways of encountering Christ's presence in the world. He does this in two ways.

First, he highlights motifs from the Gospels that will help identify the presence of Christ in the world. So, for example, he argues that 'wherever people suffer innocently or for a just cause', one can expect to find the presence of Christ, for

---

Rause, *Why God Won't Go Away: Brain Science and the Biology of Belief*, New York: Ballantine Books, 2002.

44 Drane, *Do Christians Know How to Be Spiritual?*, p. 57.

45 Clive Marsh, *Christ in Practice: A Christology of Everyday Life*, London: Darton, Longman & Todd, 2006.

we have seen this at the centre of the gospel story. Likewise, wherever 'forgiveness occurs', or 'wherever truth is told, however painful truth-telling may sometimes be' there is Christ. Wherever 'abuse of power is being challenged', or 'creativity blossoms', or 'people renounce reliance on wealth' – these are the places where Christ may be said to be present and may be encountered. Of course, this view might also be accused of leaning towards a unidirectional way of working. It is a Christian reading of the world and it is only because we attend to the gospel (especially the Gospel narratives) that we know what we are looking for and can celebrate finding these occurrences in the life of the world. But there is a difference. God is assumed to be in many places in the world, apart from the Church, even if we need to be sensitized to make the discovery. And more is required. For meeting these Christ-filled occasions invites our participation, our support, our solidarity, our prayers and our action, as well as willingness to see and tell. We have to venture forth in our everyday life with openness to the possibility that we may meet Christ, with the humility that we may not be the source or agent of this discovery and with the faith-willingness to participate, sometimes at personal cost.

The second way in which Marsh looks for Christ's presence in the world is in 'communities of practice'. This term is taken from the work of social theorists, in particular the work of Etienne Wenger, and refers to intentional communities where people are formed. Communities of practice are known by particular features: they contain and generate energy; they are interactive; they grow out of practice and meet when they need to; and while they are communities, not networks, and thus have boundaries with insiders and outsiders, they bring outcomes that are additional to their main purpose. At their best, they form people and enable them to flourish. Marsh then examines five particular communities of practice – work, education, family, friends and church – to explore how one might recognize and reflect on the presence of Christ in each of these places. This is not simply mapping and he is not naïve or idealistic about any of these communities of social interactions. They can all be destructive and fail. But when working well they also offer insights into the nature of being human, which resonate deeply with the gospel and can help us extend our understanding of God and God's ways with the world. Indeed, sometimes the insights that we gain from close attention to these communities of practice helps to refine and reform our theological thinking. His persuasive case lies in chapter 5, where having argued that peer-group friendships may have overtaken families as the place where 'the deepest joys and disappointments can be borne, the greatest risks taken and trusts expressed', he proceeds to explore what the central confession 'Jesus is Lord' looks like when the best experiences of friendship are an interpretative tool. Rather than a distant, all-powerful Lord who looks down on all creation, as was portrayed in some Christendom art work, it may mean something like our allegiance and tenacious commitment to one who stands alongside us and loves us in our strength and weakness. Thus, we have an example of learning from Christ in the world, which works its way into our thinking and speaking about Christ and God.

More provocatively, Marsh sees the Church not so much as *the* body of Christ but as *a* body of Christ, allowing there to be other ways of Christ being known in the sociality of the world. This is in part because he wants to talk of the Church as a social institution (one among, at least, five communities of practice). Thus, he tends to concentrate on the local church rather than the universal Church, as more concrete and observable. Over against the tendency for church to be seen as the only place for finding God or knowing the Christian story, Marsh wants the Church to be conceived of as a strategic and interpretative social institution. He sees the Church not so much as containing everything in itself but as a key facilitating agency providing interplay between church and other forms of social interaction. In other words, in its worship and education the Church becomes a sensitizing and reflective context for mission. The Church is to be missiological 'not in the sense that a believer brings Christ from church to the world, but rather by the believer's seeking to celebrate, with believer and non-believer alike, where Christ in social form already is'.[46]

Whether or not one agrees with the detail of Marsh's argument, the broad approach seems admirable. He wants to place the Church truly in a context of a missionary God who is at work in the world. The Church and Christian disciples are alerted to the nature of God through the revelation in Jesus, but find Christ not confined to the Church but alive in the world, working his ways in particular places and ready to be discovered and joined. At one point he quotes Dan Hardy writing about the Apostle Paul's concern 'to discover the presence of the Risen Christ in the world itself'. Just as the missionary Paul's experience was *a constant finding of Christ*,[47] so it should be for the missionary Church of the twenty-first century. What is more, by suggesting that these communities of practice are arenas where we might encounter Christ, and encouraging us to look for him there, he is speaking to the majority of followers of Christ in that he recognizes that 'most of human living is not, in fact lived as "church"'.[48] The world is thus not the place into which we foray solely to do battle, to try to gain ground or to win converts for Christ but the very place where one may be formed by Christ into the human persons we are called to be, and where we can witness God's transformative power. By attending to the Christian story, the Church helps us to see, to find grace and to discover the confidence to take risks. It will also be the place of gathering our experiences, reflecting on and interpreting them, and thus being better able to worship and to engage with God's world. Mission in this framework is, then, truly noticing what God is doing and joining in.

---

46 Marsh, *Christ in Practice: A Christology of Everyday Life*, p. 128.

47 D. W. Hardy, *God's Ways with the World: Thinking and Practising Christian Faith*, Edinburgh: T&T Clark, 1996.

48 Marsh, *Christ in Practice: A Christology of Everyday Life*. p. 15.

Disciples of the missionary God

The *missio Dei* and the Trinitarian God we proclaim is both exciting and unnerving. Exciting for it is, I think, a picture of God which speaks to us profoundly at the beginning of the twenty-first century. It tells us that the God spoken of in the scriptures and seen in Jesus is a God of loving involvement in the life of the world, at the very heart of its joy and pain, found in its creative energy, its sacrificial living and aching in the midst of its harrowing pain and destruction. This God will form and transform us as we are part of the Church's willing response to join in God's mission, and in our individual encounters in the midst of everyday living. This God is the God of the gathered and dispersed Church who calls the Church to take risks in its life and outreach and calls disciples to live in openness, alert for and attentive to his presence in the world. It promises that we are to be formed as persons in relationship with God through Christ and it also gives directions and permission to the Church to be formed anew and in different ways.

At the same time, this picture is unnerving because the risks and costs of discipleship are high. As we shall see later and in more detail, discipleship requires of us vulnerability and willingness to enter the dark and unknown places of our world both to witness to Christ and to find him. The God who is seen in this picture is a God who is never still, always moving and engaging and unwilling to allow the sin and suffering that constantly threatens life to have the last word. Rather, God is already in the hard places, experiencing the alienation but kindling love and prompting transformation. This God calls us to join in. Disciples are those who hear and respond to this God and seek to imitate the way of Jesus for now.

If our desire to affirm this broader view of the *missio Dei* is correct there are some pressing questions for disciples. How do we go about discerning the presence of God in the life of the world? How do we witness to the truth we have found with appropriate integrity, and yet with humility and openness? Is it possible to be both prophetic, counter-cultural and at the same time affirm people as made in the image of God and respect their spirituality? How much time should one spend in the gathered Church seeking God and how much in other parts of the world God loves? What are the resources for discerning God's presence and how do we use them aright? How do we handle controversy and disagreement in our discerning and reflection? What form of Christian spirituality can best sustain such a discipleship?

All these issues are to do with the practice of discipleship and it is to this that we must now turn in the next chapter.

4

The Rhythm of Discipleship

The cover picture and title of a book published in 2005 were particularly striking. The title of the book was *Fragmented Faith?* and its contents conveyed the findings of an investigation into the faith and practice of *Church Times* readers.[1] It explored some of the differences of belief held by this group of Christians – what the authors called the fault lines of faith – especially in relation to issues of sexuality, social responsibility and church practice. The title of the book was written:

FRA G MENT
ED FAITH?

Meanwhile the cover picture was a photograph of a church cut up into four pieces and deliberately placed slightly out of line with each other, like parts of a jigsaw not yet moved into position. It was a particularly eye-catching cover and very effective, not simply because it illustrated the title in a graphic form but also because as you look at the picture your eyes want to bring the four parts of the photograph into line. Implicitly the design expresses a sense of dissonance and a desire for coherence, which people feel when different parts of life, belief and practice are not consistent.

For many Christian disciples, this is the reality of everyday life in the home, community, work and nation. They are more aware of the discrepancies and inconsistencies between their professed faith and their lived experience than they are of the continuity and coherence of their discipleship.

---

1 Leslie J. Francis, Mandy Robins and Jeff Astley, *Fragmented Faith*, Milton Keynes: Paternoster, 2005.

The frustration is sometimes expressed in terms of the failure of others as well as oneself in not being able to express in structural and concrete reality the values of faith. This is how Anita Roddick put it:

> I am still looking for the modern-day equivalent of those Quakers who ran successful businesses, made money because they offered honest products and treated people decently, worked hard themselves, spent honestly, saved honestly, gave honest value for money, put back more than they took out and told no lies. The business creed, sadly, seems long forgotten.[2]

Here is another person speaking of the experience of a life divided into very different worlds with different expectations and values:

> At work I am called upon to be innovative, creative and participative; at church to be passive, conforming and controlled.
>
> At work I am required to identify my strengths and seek recognition; at church to confess my weakness and claim forgiveness.
>
> At work there is often conflict, if not always of the aggressive kind; at church conflict is denied or suppressed.
>
> At work the role of the professional is being severely questioned; at church professionals are imbued with almost mystical powers.
>
> Work demands intense periods of intellectual and/or physical activity; church places emphasis on being rather than doing, on silence, contemplation and reflection.
>
> Work puts a value on logical thought convincingly articulated; the spiritual life has a point at which logic must cease and words are shown to be the dangerous things they are.
>
> Work demands 'performance measures' and is concerned with 'outcomes'; church puts emphasis on doing one's best and leaving the outcome to God.

---

2 Anita Roddick, *Body and Soul*, New York: Crown Publications, 1991.

Of course there are jobs which require quiet reflection, some bureaucratic work environments, and some enterprising churches. But my main point is that the culture of the church and the culture of working life are so different as to create a barrier which few are motivated to remove.[3]

For many people this is what the life of a disciple is like. It is busy, demanding, complex and confusing. Trying to make meaningful links, let alone coherent sense of our mix of experiences is difficult. Indeed, as Green indicates, relating work to church and Christian life is perplexing to the point of seeming to be in parallel worlds in each of which we play different characters. And this is not only encountered in going between church and work. People experience the same difficulty in relation to making the connection between faith, on the one hand, and family, culture, leisure, politics, ethical issues and community, on the other. As I suggested in Chapter 2, this multiplicity of disparate worlds with their patterns of human relations, practices and values poses a problem for most human beings and a particular challenge for Christians.

There are two understandable but unacceptable ways of responding to the challenge. The first is to hold everything apart and keep the different parts of our lives separate. This compartmentalizing of our lives allows us to live each part in a sealed sphere where we survive by adapting to the norms, patterns and expectations in each world. We go to work, we engage with family, we vote or campaign, we attend church. We live our lives episodically and disconnectedly but at least we know how to act in each compartment, and we have some semblance of coherence as long as we don't think too hard about how it all fits together. It is easy to see why we do this but, it is dangerous psychologically because we risk being not one self but many selves, creating a loose or even unstable sense of who we are. The increase in mental illness may have much to do with this divided sense of person, being different and

3 L. Green, 'The Two Cultures', a report from *Christians in Public Life*, Birmingham, 1992.

acting differently in different places. From the point of view of faith, this way of coping is not healthy either, for it risks God being confined to the 'religious' part of lives and not having anything to do with these other 'secular' worlds. Then God is no longer creator and sustainer of the world, active in its life, but a God who operates only in church activities, and I cannot grow into God's purpose and likeness away from church community because God is confined to the religious sphere of my many worlds.

The other equally problematic way to respond to the threat of chaos that this confusion poses is to attempt to make everything conform to a religious world view. This approach is also understandable. The person who does this is in effect saying, the most important sense of self is my faith-self and everything else must be seen in the light of that commitment. It is the primary identity, so that disciples seek to impose faith language and practices into all other parts of lives, viewing these other worlds as needing to be brought into line with faith. In its more extreme form this leaves little room for growth and development, for, as we have seen, such a mission-oriented approach risks seeing all other life-spheres simply as fields for evangelism or battlefields for resisting evil, with little sensitivity and openness to God present and active within the whole of life. All issues have set answers, usually worked out in advance, and witness is practised with minimal compassion. Ultimately this is a form of arrogance that implicitly says that there is nothing to be learned of God from other sources, and can lead to the fundamentalist mindset that condones strategies inimical to the faith proclaimed. This seems to have been Jesus' objection to the Pharisees. The Pharisees clearly applied principles to every part of their lives, but in at least some cases this closed them rather than opened them to the life of God. When Jesus tells the story of the Pharisee and the publican (Luke 18.10–14) it appears that the godly habits of the Pharisee (twice-weekly fasting and tithing) have not kept him in touch with the character of God but rather have become a source of pride and a way of shutting God out. As a result, the Pharisee doesn't really know the character of God. The publican, who honestly throws himself on the divine mercy, is in reality much closer to God.

Neither of these responses helps us to be disciples in a way that fits with the view of God we outlined in the last chapter. We need to look for a better way of being whole and integrated human beings and people of faith.

The rhythm of discipleship

In looking for an answer we turn to a more dynamic and dialectical way of ordering our lives, one that does not separate and seal the compartments of our experience and does not see our non-church lives as devoid of God and needing colonization. This alternative way I call the 'rhythm of discipleship' and it is built on the idea of working with the natural rhythms of our world.

We are already familiar with the notion of natural rhythms in our daily lives. Most people still structure their day around the rising and setting of the sun, even if we do live in a 24/7 world. The seasons still affect what we wear and when we go on holiday, even if these are also shaped by the fashion and travel industries and the choices are greater. Our body rhythms strongly influence our moods and interests and we tend towards trouble when we ignore them or disregard them altogether.

The difference between a routine and a rhythm is that while the former attempts to impose order and direction on reality, the latter seeks to discern and work with an already existing, living pattern. Both bring regularity and structure but a rhythm is in tune with a movement outside itself, a tempo rooted within reality in which there is a natural flowing of energy. The Church has worked with rhythm in developing the cycle of the Christian year, allowing the moving of the earth around the sun to illuminate and give depth to the Christian seasons and festivals. So Advent looking forward to the coming of the Light is effective on dark November nights, Lent as a time of abstinence is apt in February when the earth is at its least fruitful, and Easter as the celebration of resurrection is evocative when new life is springing up in the earth, at least in the Northern hemisphere where the Christian year was created. There may, however, be another rhythm around which disciples may form their lives and that is the gathering and dispersing of the people of God.

The rhythm of discipleship, kingdom and God

In the Church of England Report entitled *All are Called*,[4] Ruth Etchells outlined what she called a theology of the laity. She began with Jesus' somewhat contrasting views of the kingdom of God. Sometimes, according to Jesus, the kingdom is obvious for all to see, like a city on a hill or a lamp placed on a lamp stand to give light to everyone in the house. Sometimes, however, Jesus tells us that the kingdom is hidden. It is like leaven in bread, active but invisible, like salt unseen but bringing out flavour, or like a tiny mustard seed almost imperceptible on the hand but able to grow into a mighty tree. In this second set of analogies, to all intents and purposes the kingdom is unnoticed and yet it is in its very hidden-ness that its power to transform reality resides. While the city on the hill enables the traveller to get her bearings, and the lamp allows people to see and act in its light, the leaven, salt and seed are most effective when mixed together with other things and their unseen presence is powerful to change the reality of which they are part. These contrasting, paradoxical aspects of the kingdom, she argued, are reflected in the Church. The Church, of course, is not the same as kingdom, but as a sign and instrument of the kingdom the Church bears something of the same character. Sometimes its life is visible and obvious, particularly when it gathers for worship in a public place, or when it develops some local project under the name of the Church or when regionally or nationally it campaigns for some cause. At other times the Church's life is hidden, unseen in the life of the world, when Christians are about their everyday business of work, home and family life, school, leisure, shopping, community involvement and politics.

---

4 *All Are Called*, London: CIO Publications (Church House), 1985.

This is the same Church, she insists, but in different forms, sometimes gathered and sometimes dispersed.

To grasp this core idea is important because even for most Christians, let alone most others, church seems to exist only when it is gathered, public and visible in its buildings or meetings. We still talk about 'going to church', our 'involvement with church' and 'raising money for the church', which suggest that it is like any other social organization that we can belong to and give some of our time and energy to. If we view the Church like this, then what appears to be important is the organized life of the gathered Church, its worship services, its ministry, its weekly activities and councils. But the dispersed Church of Christians in the life of the world is just as much the Church. It is in a different form – scattered, invisible and unnoticed by others – but profoundly about the same thing, namely responding to the reality of God made known in Jesus and sharing the good news with others. Recognizing that you are part of the Church on Monday at your desk, or playing with your children, or raising funds for your primary school or seeking employment, as well as on Sunday when you are involved in worship, is of the utmost significance because it alters the way you see yourself and what you are alert to in the world. In a later book on the same topic,[5] Etchells develops the notion of visible and hidden as key to a theology of the people of God by rooting it not only in Jesus' teaching about the kingdom but in the very character of God who is sometimes open and sometimes hidden, even for those of faith. The point she wants to make is that there is a pattern in the nature of the kingdom and in the life of God to which the gathering and dispersing of the Church corresponds. In other words, there is a deep and powerful rhythm for the Church to live its life in tune with the heart and life of God.

For disciples then the flow from one form of the Church into another and back again is to be experienced as a regular movement defining and shaping their lives. Whether it is weekly

5 Ruth Etchells, *Set My People Free: A Lay Challenge to the Churches*, London: Harper Collins, 1999.

assembling or a more or less frequent event, disciples will meet with other Christians in some form. Whether the meeting is in Sunday worship and mid-week fellowship groups of inherited church or in the innovative patterns of Fresh Expressions of church, whether it be in a large church congregation or in a cell, it will represent the gathered Christian community, the Church that comes together as a vital part of the rhythm of its life before dispersing its members back to the various places and tasks to which they are called. In the dispersed form of church Christians address the individual worlds of their daily lives where their faith will not necessarily be visible to others but where it is nevertheless at work in and through them. Then they will reassemble to share the good news discovered in the world, to be reminded of the great truths of revelation and bring the concerns of the world before God. The coming together, dispersing and coming together again is the primary rhythm of the Church and the disciples of Jesus.

It is possible to see this movement as simply part of the way we have organized our lives or fitted in with other large patterns of social life, but disciples can embrace this rhythm of gathering and dispersing as the central, defining pattern around which to form our lives. When we do, we have a sense of being in tune with God who is both open and hidden, whose love is active in the life of the world and the Church, and whose kingdom is sometimes hidden and sometime visible. There is here a deep divine resonance that allows us to live life to the full and be shaped by the vibrant life-giving rhythm of God.

If we enter this rhythm, it changes how we see ourselves and how we operate in our daily lives. There are some features of discipleship that gain meaning.

1 Vocation: Disciples are 'sent'

A visitor to a Quaker meeting sat in silence waiting for something to happen and then asked a neighbour when the service would start. 'When the worship ends' was the reply.

This sentiment is caught for many other denominations in the communion service, Eucharist or mass, which in most traditions

ends with the words 'Go in peace to love and serve the Lord.'
One of my colleagues points out that people very rarely 'go'
at that point. Often people will stay and talk together or have
coffee or speak with the minister or priest or engage in some
other activity in the church building. I guess that to line up the
words with the action you would need to say them as people
literally left the place. That could be achieved by ensuring that
everyone left at the same time or by someone standing at the
exit door and saying the words to each person individually.
While it might be effective for a time to try one or both of these
devices, I don't advocate it as a permanent liturgical pattern.
The point my friend wants to make, however, is a very strong
one. When we move from gathered to dispersed mode we do
so as sent people, people commissioned by God, who go out to
find and work with the missionary God at large in the world.

The Christian idea of being sent is a profound one. So much
so that we have a sense of being sent to the place we have
always lived or where we were going anyway. I met someone
I had known some years before at a retreat weekend. In the
time since I had last seen him he had contracted a disease that
affected his legs and he could no longer walk. He got about in a
wheelchair and with the help of others. The conference was the
furthest he had ventured for some time. Mostly he was confined
to his home or its near environs with the exception of a once
per week visit to the hospital for investigations, as they still had
not fully diagnosed the condition. His trips to the hospital were
by taxi and the same Muslim taxi driver picked him up and
brought him home each week. They had begun conversation,
which had gradually grown into a friendship and they regularly
talked about their respective faiths and asked one another for
prayer support. My friend told me that he believed that God
had 'sent him' to this person and that he was sharing his faith
and receiving a great deal at the same time. Of course, it would
be possible to say that meeting of these two happened through
the ordinary circumstances of the illness and the locality of my
friend's home. He certainly did not mean that God had somehow connived to make him ill and then fixed the taxi rota so

that this particular man turned up to transport him. He was fully aware that this meeting was a product of the chances and choices inherent in our contingent world. Rather he carried with him a deep sense of 'sentness'. He believed that in his everyday life he was sent by God and he was working with God in the place he happened to find himself.

It is through this sense of being sent that many people discover a personal vocation in God's purposes. Some people would use the word vocation to speak about their job or career or perhaps about their care of their family or involvement in local politics. They mean that they have a calling to give their time and energy, passions and gifts to serve in that particular sphere. This is where they are sent and what they have to do. The Latin roots of the word from which we get vocation means 'calling out' or 'calling forth'. Individuals may experience a calling out from what they are doing currently to another direction or career. Alternatively, they may experience a calling forth of response and a life commitment in the place God has already put them.

These are appropriate uses of the word vocation, very much in line with how Calvin and Luther used the term. We ought to exercise caution with this word, however. In a society where some work is still exploitative and some experiences of ordinary living are degrading, we need to be careful before baptizing everyone's daily experience with the word vocation, simply because they are disciples. That does not mean that in any of those settings one cannot carry a sense that one is there to work with God, perhaps especially to express love and support, to resist dehumanizing, to seek for justice or simply to offer a smile to help fellow strugglers survive. In much discussion of vocation the emphasis is on choosing a path, a role or career to serve God[6] but the only choice open for some people may be how, not whether, to live in this way. Vocation in this context is the fundamental vocation of all Christians to be with God and in practice will mean owning that it is a place where

6 See, for example, Douglas J. Brouwer, *What Am I Supposed to Do with My Life?*, Grand Rapids and Cambridge: Eerdmans, 2006.

God shares people's experience and wants us with him to bring some light and hope. Charles Elliot's translation of the beatitudes is apt here.[7] The words 'blessed are', he suggests, might be best understood if translated 'you are in the right place when', for example: you are in the right place when you are poor (or among the poor), or when you mourn (or are among those who are hurting), or you are in the right place when you (are among those who) hunger and thirst for righteousness. All these places are places of God's blessing because God is there. For some people their demoralizing and demeaning work or their situation of low expectations, neglect and deprivation may be a place to be with God. Those who choose to see their situation in this way and actively live in the reality of God's presence are sharing in God's mission and participating in the vocation of God's people.

It may be better to say that our calling as the people of God may grow into a personal vocation, as our serving of God is taken up willingly and it also engages our gifts and experiences, our commitments and passions and for which our life is deliberately oriented and shaped. Those who know that they are sent are on the way to discovering their personal vocation within the vocation of all God's people.

2 Formation: Disciples are shapers being shaped

Sharing in God's mission, being co-creators, being alert to signs of the kingdom requires active involvement. Those who participate in the rhythm of discipleship are dispersed to be actors in the great drama, not audiences watching the performance.

Thus, disciples are to shape the world and its life. Such active participation can take many forms. I recently met a young Christian and a young Muslim who were both good table-tennis players and who had together started a club for disabled youngsters to learn the sport. I don't think faith was discussed between them, nor was it an explicit part of the thinking about starting the club, but both realized that such a good sport,

---

7 See Charles Elliot, *Praying the Kingdom*, London: Darton, Longman & Todd, 1985.

although theoretically available to anyone, offered little by way of coaching and training for those with impairment. So they went on coaching courses to offer the best support and training for their club members. A couple of weeks afterwards, I noticed an article about a young teenage girl in a wheelchair from the same area who was about to take part in national table-tennis championships. I don't know whether she belonged to their club or not but it was clear to me that these two were part of creating a world in which such a person could find and develop their skill to national level.

Disciples also shape the world by challenging taken-for-granted values. I heard about Edith from an American professor visiting Durham. She was (and maybe still is) a modestly paid administrative worker in a university department. Her reputation in the department was of being a dedicated, hardworking, caring and pleasant person who helped the faculty do its work to the best of her ability. For those who asked, she would tell them she was a Christian, but for the most part her faith quietly informed her work. Then there was a scandal. She was investigated by the Inland Revenue Service. It seems that they could not believe the level of her gift-aided giving over the course of the year. They thought there might be money laundering or something equally sinister going on behind the apparently very generous giving. The truth was, however, exactly as it was presented. She believed she had enough to live on and gave the rest away to a wide range of charities. When all this came out, the effect on those around her who earned twice, three and four times as much, was profound. The visiting professor said 'I have never been investigated by the IRS because I gave too much away! Have you?' By her attitude and action Edith was being counter-cultural in a small but effective way.

Occasionally our action to shape the world is on a grand scale. Anyone who saw the film *Amazing Grace* could not but be struck by the way a small diverse group of men and women, not just William Wilberforce, were engaged to reshape both culture and practice in British society. Their efforts were stretched over many years and progress was only very slowly made because of the vested interests in maintaining the prevailing values. Only after many years did a new and better view come to be. A similar story could be told of those who began the Fairtrade movement in our own time. These major changes often take a long time and determined, active commitment to accomplish.

On the other hand, small acts can be very effective also. I have a memory of watching Donald Sinden perform in a play put on by the Royal Shakespeare Company. At one moment in the play he simply looked at the audience and changed the expression on his face. It took less than a couple of seconds and, of course, many of us were at some distance from the stage but so effective was this small movement that the whole audience moved with him from one mood to its opposite. Etchells talks about the primary work of the people of God in the world as believing.[8] She means by this retaining the same view of God as loving, trustworthy and working to redeem the world wherever we are and in whatever circumstance we find ourselves. It is here that simply believing can transform the landscape. Mark Green records this story:

> Emily, a small Chinese lady, works at the United Nations. One day one of her co-workers, a fairly large lady, wasn't feeling well.
> 'Can I get you a cup of tea?' Emily enquired.
> 'No,' the other replied rather shortly. 'I don't drink the teas here. I only drink camomile.'
> Emily left her, quietly slipped on her coat, took the lift down several floors and went to a nearby shop. She returned with a box of camomile tea and gave it in her small hand to this large lady, who immediately enveloped her in a huge hug, exclaiming, 'Emily I love you'.
> Emily replied, rather muffled from the epicentre of this massive hug, 'I love you too.'[9]

---

8 Etchells, *Set My People Free*, p. 95.
9 M. Greene, *Thank God It's Monday*, Bletchley: Scripture Union, 1994, p. 49.

Clearly this simple act made a big difference.

All these stories are about being active shapers of the world but there is another dimension to all of this. Those who act to make and influence the world in which they live are also shaped by their actions. You cannot act in love and care towards your neighbours without being changed, you cannot fight for justice in a detached way and not be affected by the cause and its reality. Our deeds and our character are related. We become what we live. What is more, as we suggested in the previous chapter, God meets us in the world and is forming and shaping us through our encounters. As Clive Marsh argued,[10] wherever people suffer innocently or for a just cause, one can expect to find the presence of Christ, wherever forgiveness occurs or truth is told, however painful truth-telling may sometimes be, there is Christ. Wherever abuse of power is being challenged or creativity blossoms, or people renounce reliance on wealth, these are the places where Christ may be said to be present and may be encountered and through these epiphanies is moulding us for purpose.

But how do we know we are shaping things in the right ways and what do we do when our flawed humanity and individual weaknesses undermine what we intend or add to the destructive tendencies of society? How do we recognize the God who is meeting and forming us in the life of the world? This is where the rhythm of discipleship is vital. For gathering together as church is precisely in order to be honest about our sins; to revisit the gospel in scripture, preaching and sharing; to find forgiveness; to catch a fresh vision of God; and to meet God in the worship life of the gathered Church. This too is powerful for forming us. The words of the preaching opening up scripture, the testimony of human and yet godly people pointing to change and renewal, the honest offering of our prayers, the simple yet profound encounter with the truth of God as we share bread and wine; all these are forming and transformative of our lives.

10 See Clive Marsh, *Christ in Practice: A Christology of Everyday Life*, London: Darton, Longman & Todd, 2006.

Ephesians 4.11–16 gives insight into this formational process:

> The gifts he gave were that some would be apostles, some prophets, some evangelists, some pastors and teachers, to equip the saints for the work of ministry, for building up the body of Christ, until all of us come to the unity of the faith and of the knowledge of the Son of God, to maturity, to the measure of the full stature of Christ. We must no longer be children, tossed to and fro and blown about by every wind of doctrine, by people's trickery, by their craftiness in deceitful scheming. But speaking the truth in love, we must grow up in every way into him who is the head, into Christ, from whom the whole body, joined and knit together by every ligament with which it is equipped, as each part is working properly, promotes the body's growth in building itself up in love.

The gifts of God to the Church are apostles, prophets, evangelists, teachers and preachers and the purpose of these gifts is to build up (or form) the body of Christ and to bring maturity, making us more like Christ. These gifts come into play in the gathered Church where pastors, teachers and prophets are recognized and given space to exercise their ministry. Even with apostles and evangelists, whose gifts may be intended for carrying the messages to those away from the gathered Church, their knowledge and insights are offered when the community gathers. This enriching by the gifts of the gathered community is also seen in 1 Corinthians 12 and in Romans 12, though in both cases the gifts spill over beyond the gathered life. The fundamental intention of this gathering of gifts is to edify and strengthen. As Paul puts it later in his letter to Corinth, 'When you come together, each one has a hymn, a lesson, a revelation, a tongue, or an interpretation. Let all things be done for building up' (1 Corinthians 14.26).

We are thus formed by the community and by the presence of God among the gathered people of God.

The passage in Ephesians 4 reaches its climax in verse 16

where we are 'to grow up in every way into him who is the head, into Christ'. There is a wonderfully ambiguous set of Greek words here, so that it is possible to translate this verse in another way as 'we are to cause all things to grow in Christ who is the head'. One translation implies that the purpose of all that is going on in earlier verses of Ephesians 4 is to enable us to grow into Christ. The other suggests that all these are directed towards us causing all things to grow into the shape of Christ. All things here might include relationships, work, family, structures of society and politics, which through our actions begin to take a Christ-like pattern and form. Scholars tend to prefer the first translation, but it is possible that the author, like a good writer, knew that sometimes you can say two things in one sentence. If so, this verse is suggesting that shaping and being shaped are not separate processes but that as we are shaping the world in which we live according to Christ, so also we are being shaped into his likeness by our encounters with him in the world and in the gathered Church.

So then disciples are being shaped in the rhythm of gathering and dispersing. It is not simply in the gathered Church that we are formed into Christ-like-ness, nor in the business of making and shaping the world. It is in the continuing movement between gathered and dispersed, our worship and our work that we are fashioned by God. Participating in the rhythm of gathering and dispersing puts us into an interactive dynamic relationship, overflowing with energy, that is person forming and reality shaping at the same time.

3 Translation: Disciples are bilingual

Moving between different forms of being church is like moving between two different countries, cultures and languages. Words and phrases that would be normal and clear in the context of the gathered Church may not be intelligible in the post-religious worlds of work, social and public life. If you don't believe me, stand outside the school gate with parents collecting their children and start up a conversation on the grace of God, or fellowship, or the incarnation. I use these words because they are commonly known and used among most Christians. (There are more obscure theological terms that would make the conversation even more difficult!) It is no easy matter and it can feel like suddenly switching into Polish or French in the middle of an English conversation.

Living with two languages is not easy. People sometimes complain about 'churchy' language, asking for it to be updated or dropped altogether so that those unfamiliar with church or Christian faith can understand. We need, they argue, to be able to explain in terms that people will understand and build bridges to the life-worlds of non-Christians. Seeker services deliberately work at making access to faith language as easy as possible, as does popular apologetics. On the other hand, there is often a deep resistance apparent the moment people introduce the discourse of their workplace or office to the church context. Speak of efficiency or value for money or market forces, for example, and hackles may rise in the church council or Bible study group.

There is, however, a deeper problem that neither of these protagonists recognizes. Languages are more than sets of words that are roughly the equivalents of the words in other languages. They carry ideas and assumptions about the world, how it is ordered and run, what constitutes knowledge and what is of ultimate meaning. Wittgenstein famously argued that the way the language game is constructed determines what can be enacted and accomplished. Philosophers such as Foucault and social theorists such as Habermas have argued that languages (or discourses) are not neutral but have power interests which are embedded in them. Thus, it may not be possible simply to replace one language with another or translate everything without remainder into other discourses. That doesn't mean we can't make Christian ideas clearer using everyday language or accept some insights from other language worlds. It remains, however, important that the language of faith is available to us to explore the depth of God, and that we can know and use the everyday language of the other worlds in which we live.

Walter Brueggemann helps us here with a creative exegesis

of 2 Kings 18.[11] In the story of Sennacherib's armies about to crush Jerusalem, the spokesmen for the Assyrian army attempt to speak in Hebrew, but Israel's negotiators wish them to speak in Aramaic – the dominant language of empire and trade at the time. Judah's leaders are willing to speak Aramaic on the wall with the invaders but speak Hebrew behind the wall with their people. According to Brueggemann, preserving the language of the Hebrew faith here allows people to explore the world from their faith perspective. To let it go is to concede that there is no alternative way of looking at reality and thus accept the invaders' view, a view that excludes the reality of God. Without the possibility of thinking and speaking in our faith language we also lose the critical edge that enables us to see, challenge and change constructions of reality which may be degrading and damaging to human beings.

Disciples are thus called to be bilingual, to speak two languages and to reflect on the places where they match and mismatch. We don't impose our faith language on our workplace or community or leisure club inappropriately. Rather, we become fluent in the language that is common and used in these places. We seek to understand how things are perceived and described and engaged within these worlds, but because we can speak another language – the language of Christian faith – we have the potential to infuse the secular language with new meaning and assumptions, to confront harmful ideas and make creative connections between the two worlds. Another of my current colleagues describes knowing the biblical world as like learning a foreign language, entering a world that is quite different from the one with which we are familiar and where the reality is conceived of and described differently. He says that when you become confident in the language (when you can 'speak Bible', as it were) you begin to think and act differently in your everyday world. Your words and ways become infected by the language of faith.

---

11 Walter Brueggemann, 'The Legitimacy of a Sectarian Hermeneutic', in *Interpretation and Obedience*, ed. Walter Brueggemann, Minneapolis: Fortress Press, 1991.

By being fluent in two languages disciples also become inter-
preters to and from the gathered Church, able to help the
Church understand reality as it is seen and experienced by people in particular spheres of life and also able to translate their
faith into the everyday speech of their work and home. What
is more, bilingual disciples can bring words, images and metaphors from their daily lives to the faith community, enabling
the Church to add to or enrich its perception of God and
God's world. This is how our language of faith has grown and
developed from the New Testament times onwards. It brings
challenge both ways and provides the possibility of change
and growth. So in the extract at the beginning of the chapter, Green is right to contrast the languages and ideas of her
work and church. Looking at her list, there are implicit tasks
for both church and workplace and therein lies a tension with
the potential for fruitful change.

The rhythm of gathering and dispersing enables the interaction of languages and a dialogue in and through the disciples.

4   Interchange: Disciples are go-betweens

Finally, disciples who participate in the rhythm of discipleship,
as well as being people of more than one language, are also
travellers and traders. They take things into and out of gathered Church and into and out of their daily worlds. They will
have stories to tell of their journeys, some ordinary and some
extraordinary, of God's wonders encountered and experienced, which need to be heard when the company of travellers
gathers, and they will have energy, insight and gifts to carry to
the mission field. Disciples learn things that need to be known
and reflected on by the wider Christian community. They are,
to borrow the language of learning organizations, 'outworkers'
whose knowledge can change the way the organization does
its work.

Space must be made for this exchange for it is a vital part
of the movement. At one church I visited there was a regular
monthly slot where someone from the congregation would give
a brief talk on their work and their Christian faith and then

discuss with others the insights and dilemmas that were in their place of employment. At another church in their monthly café-style worship and discussion, a number of people spoke of what it was like to try and live out faith in their daily world – they included a teenager at school, a retired man, a social worker with drug addicts and an office secretary. Following the sharing, each of the table groups discussed what they had learned from the contributors and then shared their own experience of faith and everyday life. At another church there is a regular 'faith and work' group where the members meet to listen, pray for and support each other in the daily work as disciples.

These all represent practical attempts to gather the experience of the go-between disciples and to support the living of Christian faith in everyday life. But they also enrich the church's authentic worship life. As Ruth Etchells puts it:

> The church's community of worship and belief only gains its real power when we bring with us our 'solidarity' with the world which we carry in our hearts[12]

By bringing the deep concerns of our everyday worlds together there is spiritual dynamic which infuses and transforms our situations.

> That is why, though gathering together with fellow believers can be a resting place, a refreshment and solace, its real power is never fully effective until it is allowed to play on, probe and irradiate those concerns of the world which are each lay person's given territory.[13]

Of course, there is a flow the other way also. The gathered Christian community will by its exploration of the word, its bonds of fellowship and its experience of God equip people to see things in a different way. It may be that for the short time

---

12 Etchells, *Set My People Free*, p. 133.
13 Etchells, *Set My People Free*, p. 134.

of gathering and worship we live by another story and so get all stories into perspective and give them direction.

The balance is not easy to achieve. In describing the highly successful small group work of Willow Creek church, Robinson and Donahue say that groups need to focus on both 'life experience' (what issues people bring from their lives) and 'truth' (the gospel as revealed). In their experience, it is easy to lean towards one of those at the expense of the other. Groups, they say, can easily be truth focused and thus content driven with the result that people have many 'right' answers but little application. Alternatively, they can be life focused and experience driven, which results in an emphasis on supporting people but not engaging with the truth of the faith. Neither produces the transformation to which Christ calls us. That is only achieved when the truths of the faith are in dialogue with our life experience. When that happens they say that 'meetings become moments' – occasions when all are enriched through the love of God at work in Church and world and located in the lives of the disciples gathered.[14]

A spiritual rhythm

Entering into the rhythm of discipleship is a powerful and exciting adventure. It resonates with the life of God and the reality of God's kingdom and it draws us into life-giving work of the missionary God. In this rhythm we discover ourselves 'sent' and find our personal vocation; we are active in shaping the world and at the same time are shaped by a relationship with God at the heart of the rhythm; and in the process we become translators, travellers and traders working continually in the ebb and flow of the Church between its gathered and dispersed life, learning, expressing, enhancing and extending the life of the Church and our understanding of God.

This rhythm has a potent spirituality, which draws from the experience of God in the gathered life of the Church and from

14 Bill Donahue and Russ Robinson, *Building a Church of Small Groups*, Grand Rapids: Zondervan, 2001.

the experience of God in the life of the world. Given that our experience flows around these two poles of God's activity one might describe it as an *elliptical spirituality*. Just as the locus of an ellipse is two points, so for disciples the reference points for their knowledge of and response to God is in two places, and as they gather or disperse these focal points will alter. So disciples move through life in the rhythm of faith and are constantly held in relationship with God and being sustained and strengthened by his love.

Elliptical spirituality

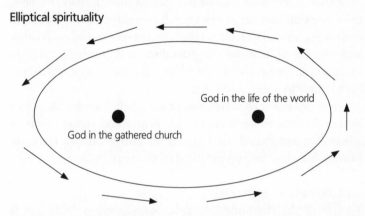

My view is that a figure of eight might be a better way of visualizing the idea and capturing the sense of the flowing of movement of the rhythm.

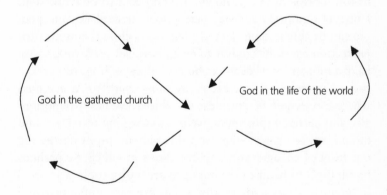

Living in the rhythm

Of course, participating in the rhythm or dance of faith requires much of us. In the first place, we need to choose to work with the rhythm, to engage our lives in this movement, to see the scope and activities of our life in this framework. Second, we need to keep God at the centre. In this movement we sometimes find God in the gathered community and sometimes in the life of the world, but it is an act of faith and commitment to keep God at the centre of our lives all the time. Finally, we need to ensure that there is in our church life, gathered or dispersed, both learning and sharing so that the two parts feed each other and support all disciples. In attending to these things, we are living in the rhythm of discipleship and experiencing the transforming partnership with God.

There are some attitudes and practices that enable us to live in this rhythm, to keep God at the centre and create forms of fellowship and church that sustain us in our calling. Here are four. A fifth one will be explored in the next chapter.

1   Courageous openness

To live in the rhythm of discipleship requires a faith that is open to the possibility of God at all times. Just as plants open themselves to the sunlight, so disciples thrive when they are open to God's grace wherever they find themselves. This kind of openness is not easy, however, and needs to be worked at. Familiar situations dull our perceptions, new places and people can be threatening. Just as plants also close themselves for protection from the cold or to defend against predators, so we have a human set of defences built up over millions of years to protect ourselves. There are many times (perhaps in one day) where our degree of openness is reduced. Mentally, emotionally and perhaps spiritually, we are less willing to receive and more ready to protect what we hold as important by decreasing our level of engagement. The situations in which we perhaps find it most difficult to remain open are with people who seem different from us and situations that are very unfamiliar and uncomfortable. In these settings we close down, become cool and unreceptive, resistant to ideas and views (even if we don't actively say so). We may even become hostile or obviously unco-operative.

It would be wrong to imply that we should take no notice of our instincts. Clearly, people have survived dangers and resisted evil and corruption by being alert to the reality of their context and closing themselves to certain ideas and behaviours. Others have suffered because they weren't so resistant. There are situations, however, where our lack of openness is more to do with our prejudices and lack of knowledge and experience than the reality of the perceived threat. It is exactly at these places where we may miss the reality of God, particularly as God comes to us through other human beings. Two Jewish theologians have drawn our attention to the need to be open to the 'otherness' in the midst of the world and especially in other human beings. Martin Buber suggested the nature of life was dialogic – in conversation and exchange – in which we find ourselves and respond to God through the openness we have to others. His influential idea of 'I–thou' relationships is that rather than treat people in an 'I–it' relationship, as if others were inanimate objects in our world, we should regard a person as a 'thou', another living being in relationship with whom we find the truth of ourselves and through whom we may glimpse God. Buber wrote: 'Every particular Thou is a glimpse to the eternal Thou.'[15]

Emmanuel Levinas speaks of the 'Other', the reality and mystery of God, being met when we turn towards the 'other', the difference and strangeness of the people we encounter in our lives. It is in being open to that which is strange, mysterious even, in others that we are confronted with that which may open and connect us to the Otherness of God.

Neither Buber nor Levinas could be accused of a romantic, unreal view of life. Buber was forced to leave Germany when Hitler rose to power and was engaged in the political debates

---

15 Martin Buber, *I and Thou*, translated by Ronald Gregor Smith, Edinburgh: T&T Clark, 1958, 2nd ed., p. 75.

and tensions of the setting up of the state of Israel. Levinas was a Holocaust survivor. Both, however, shared the deep belief that openness and a willingness to journey outwards towards others is central to meeting God.

Openness requires some discernment and courage. The very act of opening ourselves to others, especially to those who seem to be different from us, involves a degree of vulnerability. That is true at the very elementary level of venturing a question or starting up a conversation. Our openness may not be reciprocated, and we may on occasions open ourselves to things that are hard to handle. Courage is needed. The alternative to courageous openness is not to take the risk. As in the parable, we can bury our talent in the ground, so it is safe, but lose the possibility of much gain (Matthew 25.15–28). It is clear from the parable what it was that Jesus expected of his followers: risk taking! Disciples who are translators, traders and travellers need to be people of courageous openness, willing to take such risks.

2   Careful accountability

Disciples who live openly in the world will want and need to tell their stories. Like bird watchers who go to a special place to catch sight of a rare bird, they must find someone, preferably someone who shares their passion, to whom to relate their tale and to show their photos. Disciples need to give an account of their discoveries. They must talk of the God they have discerned in the life of the world and that means that the gathered Church must be a community of conversation and storytelling, where accounts can be given and understanding explored and extended. This is the first meaning of accountability – the ability to give an honest account of the experience of faith in action.

There is another meaning of the word 'accountability' in this context. This is accountability as holding up one's action and experience for inspection and scrutiny and being prepared to receive honest feedback from others on the pattern of your discipleship. Some Christians do this with a critical friend or a spiritual director with whom they seek to be honest and to whom they look to receive truthful comment and suggestion in return. Membership of some Christian communities requires this kind of accountability. For example, to be a member of the Iona Community, one must agree to live by five simple rules.[16] Three of the five rules include the word 'accounting'. Members are to account for their use of money and time and to meet together to be accountable for their commitment to prayer and action for justice. The Iona Community is an ecumenical and largely dispersed community that began in 1938, but the pattern is similar to the ancient religious orders wherein those who live within the rule of the order regularly meet with the leader or another member of the community for an honest accounting for the way they have followed or failed in their duties, commitments and inner life. Today many people join lay or tertiary orders of the Franciscans or Benedictines for their structured approach to discipleship in which they are accountable. In the early Methodist class meetings this kind of accountability was described as 'watching over one another in love' and a person was only admitted to membership of such a group if she or he could honestly say yes to the question 'Do you desire to be told your faults?' Today some cell groups function like this, as do Covenant Discipleship groups and Cursillo or Walk to Emmaus groups. All offer a structure and pattern of accountability for those who belong.

Clearly, to enter a structure or relationship of this kind there needs to be great care taken. Disciples need to have confidence that their honest sharing is safe, that all feedback from an individual or group is offered with the intention of support and to help to live the Christian live faithfully, and that power is not abused. The adjective 'careful' thus is an important accompanying word. Accountability that is not surrounded with loving care can do damage. Accountability that is care-full, however, can enable people to speak of their experiences of

---

16 The Iona Community rules are: 1. Daily Prayer and Bible-reading; 2. Sharing and accounting for the use of our money; 3. Planning and accounting for the use of our time; 4. Action for Justice and Peace in society; 5. Meeting with and accounting to each other.

God, walk more faithfully the Christian way and sense that they are journeying with others.

3 Conscientious immersion in the tradition

Openness, therefore, needs to be lived within a framework of accountability. This accountability allows stories to be communicated and explored, enables disciples to share the journey together and provides the possibility of checking with others one's own Christian lifestyle actions. Accountability is not sufficient on its own, however. Indeed the practice of accountability can only be meaningful when there are reference points against which to check responses and in relation to which we can tell stories and share experiences. Members of the Iona Community, which I mentioned above, seek to live by five simple rules. These rules are the first reference point for members but they are, themselves, distilled from the scriptures and tradition of the Church. What is more, these rules are understood and interpreted through ongoing engagement with the Bible and traditions of the church. Without a deep engagement with the sources and records of the faith it would be easy for the rules to become empty regulations and practices that are kept for their own sake and not as an aid to being faithful disciples, alive to God at work in the world.

Disciples need to be people who enter into the Bible to become familiar with God's character and ways to be able to recognize God in their travelling and trading lives of everyday work and life.

Entering into the Bible and the tradition of the Church is more than becoming familiar with facts and stories or knowledgeable about history and the issues of interpretation. It means entering with heart and mind, with imagination and passion into the living reality of the divine revelation and the human response to it in history. It means living inside the story. The Ignatian pattern of reading the scriptures catches the idea of this well. In this approach, the reader does not simply read the story as if she were an observer but seeks to enter into the story as a participant through identifying with a character in the story and engaging with the narrative from that perspective. Thus, the emotions and thoughts that might have accompanied the original incident or event are sensed, but equally important the reader's own emotions and thoughts are involved too and come into dialogue with the dynamics of the text. Although this is a practised way of reading the scriptures (and one to be tried if you have not done it) it serves here as a metaphor for what is happening in our study and engagement with the Church's tradition. We get to know the Christian story and the character of God not by amassing lots of repeatable facts and information but by entering into the faith tradition ourselves and living inside it. This is a form of immersion, letting your whole self be immersed in the reality, letting your story be caught up in God's story and allowing the Spirit room to speak to mind and heart through our engagement.

Immersion does not mean being uncritical in one's reading of the Bible or in exploring the tradition. There are lots of questions to be asked and debate to be had and much of our engagement means making judgements about previous expressions and interpretations of the faith as we are appropriating that tradition for ourselves. We will not understand it or live exactly as a previous generation, not even the first disciples who wrote the New Testament.

Again we have employed a qualifying word to the key verb 'immerse'. Conscientious here means deliberate, self-conscious and repeated engagement, study and reflection as a disciple, as an individual and with others. It means daily, weekly and life-long learning so that the witnesses of the past become the inspiration and energy for our present, so that the faults of the past alert us to possible dangers now and so that debates of the past offer us insight for today. Most of all, it is an intentional seeking to be more acquainted with the God whose character and passion are revealed in the scriptures, in the Church's history and work and most supremely in Jesus.

4   Constant prayerfulness

Continuity in the life of the disciple, whether in gathered or dispersed Church, lies in the relationship with God. God is active in the Church and the world, and the disciple, wherever she or he is found, is to be watching for God's presence and activity. This watching attitude is fundamentally one of prayerfulness. Prayerfulness here means praying but not in the mechanical sense of saying prayers at certain points in the day, maintaining a quiet time or attending prayer meetings, though these will develop prayerfulness. Rather, it means a life lived in continual conversation with God, wherein one's daily devotions and arrow prayers shot to God in moments of need or concern, melt into the flow of life itself and pervade the doing of work, everyday conversation, the generation of thought and the physical activity of movement, exercise and rest.

For prayerfulness to be genuine one needs to allow prayer to gather the whole of one's life experience. Traditionally, prayer has been spoken of in different moods – praise, adoration, confession, thanksgiving and intercession. We could perhaps add to this honest sharing of pain, anger or frustration – what in the psalms is identified as a lament – the burbling expressions of half-formed thoughts, and the almost trivial chatter that we would engage in with a close friend, which, on one level, is ephemeral and yet strengthens our intimacy and love. In the end, prayerfulness is life lived in continual relationship with God, catching up everything we are in response to God's loving openness to us.

We will return to the nurture of the faith-attitudes later in the book. For now we note that to live as disciples in the rhythm of discipleship we need to practise courageous openness, careful accountability, conscientious immersion in the tradition and constant prayerfulness that speaks to and listens to God in and through all that happens in our life and work. There is one further practice that we need to explore: what I call 'faithful reflection' within the rhythms of discipleship. This we will do as we turn to the next chapter, 'The Reflective Disciple'.

5

The Reflective Disciple

Discipleship is not easy. It requires both will and discipline and it needs to be sustained over time, like on a serious hike, where setting off down the track may be straightforward, indeed, you may be full of excitement, anticipation and confidence. Hills, unmarked paths, swollen rivers don't daunt you. You may even relish the challenge they pose. But when you have walked many miles, energy levels are low, weather conditions have deteriorated and the terrain is confusing, to see the hike through is often down to two abilities: your ability to remain disciplined in checking maps, compass and landmarks and your ability to will the next step.

The path of discipleship is made possible by God's grace. The invitation to follow Jesus is an act of God's gracious love; the possibility of taking up that invitation is facilitated by God's grace and the journey itself is sustained continually by grace. Yet at the same time, the journey calls for a personal commitment of will and our disciplined engagement with the means of grace – the places and activities where grace is made available.

Many books on our theme concentrate on what one might call the 'core disciplines of discipleship': prayer, study, fellowship, witness and the nurture of Christian virtues, such as patience, kindness, gentleness and self-control or others listed in Galatians 5.22. These books provide insight and advice on how to develop these practices and the fruitful qualities that issue from them. Take, for example, a book written over 50 years ago by a leading Methodist, Leslie Weatherhead.[1] The

1 Leslie Dixon Weatherhead, *Discipleship*, London: SCM Press, 2nd ed., 1954.

chapters of the book include titles such as 'Sharing' (about the need for and ways of confessing sin), 'Quiet Time' (the practice of daily prayer), 'Fellowship' (the value of small groups for learning and growth), and 'Guidance' (concerning how to seek God's will for one's own life). These are the disciplines or 'means of grace' that Weatherhead advocates as sustaining Christian discipleship. Likewise, David Watson, writing about discipleship in the 1980s, sets out a cluster of disciplines at the heart of Christian living. These include prayer and Bible study but also 'living a simple lifestyle', and 'the creating of community'. Watson also emphasizes engagement in the life of the Spirit, reflecting the recovery of a sense of the immediacy of the Spirit in the Charismatic movement of that period.[2]

Both these influential Christian leaders recognized the importance of embedding and embodying the call of discipleship in regular day-to-day activities that link us to God and that nurture our attentiveness to God's character and ways. They both offer good practical advice, on how to set about and develop practical devotion – times of day, useful material, checks for good interpretation. They warn us about the dangers and difficulties of certain patterns and provide advice on how to overcome these. Such detailed and proscriptive help is often crucial for structuring our lives to be disciples. We need the assistance of those who have found good and useful ways of engaging with the means of grace.

I have avoided giving detailed instruction on prayer or Bible study or lifestyle, however. Rather I have pointed towards attitudes or orientations that characterize the life of the disciples. In the previous chapter we looked at the rhythm of discipleship and the kind of qualities that living in this pattern of gathering and dispersal involves. It requires a courageous openness, a careful accountability, a conscientious immersion in the tradition and a constant prayerfulness that speaks to and listens to God in and through all that happens in our life and work. These are not simple activities or practices, which having read about one can go away and instantly perform. They are rather attitudes

---

2 David Watson, *Discipleship*, London: Hodder & Stoughton, 1981.

of mind and heart that are nurtured in a variety of ways. Of course, though, they must take concrete form to realize. They grow out of particular patterns of praying, reading the Bible, relating to other Christians and engaging with other people in the life of the world. Patterns change, however. They change because we change over time, our world changes, and our church experiences change. You can see this by comparing the two books mentioned above. Both Weatherhead and Watson draw strongly on their own experience and some particular features of their contemporary culture in advocating particular patterns. Weatherhead uses psychology (a new field in his day), his enthusiasm for the Oxford Group[3] and his own Methodist practice to suggest particular patterns of spirituality. Watson offers us much from the refreshing experience of charismatic renewal that had touched his own church and many others in the late 1970s and early 1980s to offer a formula for the practice of discipleship. These particular discipleship formulae are right and proper and ultimately unavoidable. Every attempt to sketch out a concrete pattern of Christian discipleship will only be effective if it is appropriate for its age; but, as a result, it may not work in the next. It cannot be repeated in another context or age without a degree of modification and development.

It is likely that our own age will give birth to different ways of structuring spirituality.[4] As we seek this I believe that the attitudes or qualities named above give us direction within which to develop particular practical forms of spirituality.

I do, however, advocate here one simple practice as vital to the practice of Christian discipleship, namely faithful reflection. In this chapter we will explore what this means and how it works.

---

3 The Oxford Group was a Christian movement initiated by Frank Buchman, influential in the first half of the twentieth century. It stressed personal confession and self surrender – terms which Weatherhead used a good deal.

4 See Olive M. Fleming Drane, *Spirituality to Go: Rituals and Reflections for Everyday Living*, London: Darton, Longman & Todd, 2005 for an interesting way of embedding spirituality in post-modern lifestyles.

What is faithful reflection?

Reflection is a common enough term. Indeed, in some circles it has been a buzz word for a long time. At core, reflection is about focusing on something – an experience, a text, a piece of artwork, a story, a performance, oneself even – in a way that enables learning and gives birth to new insight and knowledge. In a way, it is a form of thinking but one that is concerned with how things fit together: how we achieve coherence of thought, attitude and action; our sense of self and our view of the world; our belief and lifestyle. In that way, it is much more than the application of rational thought to a problem. Rather, it is a way of engaging our whole person with our experience of life and creating meaningful ways of living.

We shall explore the meaning of reflection in greater depth shortly but before we do let us turn to the word faithful and see what attaching the adjective faithful to the word reflection is intended to mean.

Faithful reflection

My preferred term for the core practice of discipleship is faithful reflection. Elsewhere I have written about theological reflection,[5] which is another term for the same practice. I am not using that term here for several reasons. In part it is because the word theology and its associated adjective theological are often a 'turn off'. Many people, especially those who have not had opportunity to study theology, find the words intimidating and when they hear them an expectation is aroused of something difficult or dull or both! That is not the only reason, however. Were it the only reason, I could argue that we simply need to learn to be at ease with the term, for its content and reality make learning the words worth it.

The other reasons are more positive. In many ways, the term 'faithful reflection' catches the notion better. Faithful, in

---

5 Steven Croft and Roger Walton, *Learning for Ministry*, London: Church House Publishing, 2005.

the first place, means full of faith. Thus, faithful reflection is reflection done by persons of faith. It refers to people who are seeking to make sense of (and with the help of) a faith that they already possess. Faithful reflection is practised by people who are in an active, living relationship with God. They have begun the journey of faith and are seeking to learn to live better as disciples of Christ, to exercise their faith more effectively in daily living. Let's be clear. Reflection does not make a person a Christian and neither does the study of theology, valuable though both of these are. The beginning of faith is simply trust in God. Christian faith is trust in God made known in Jesus Christ and disciples are those who have started to live in trust and are resolved to follow Jesus. Such disciples are exactly the people who engage in faithful reflection.

Second, the 'faithful' in faithful reflection refers not only to the position of faith of the reflector but also to the resources we use in the practice. Faithful reflection utilizes the faith traditions of the Church to do its work. In other words, it draws on the scriptures, the writings of Christians of the past, and the many varied ways of expressing faith that have been handed on to us in art, music, hymns, creeds, diaries, poetry, biographies and even architecture. We deliberately and intentionally bring into our reflections these stories and traditions to help connect whatever we are thinking about to the Christian faith and to let them cast light on the subject. In this way we also ensure that this kind of reflection is not an individualistic enterprise but takes place within the life and calling of the Church. One of the ways of doing and developing our reflecting is in conversation with others, whose knowledge and experience may be different from ours and thus can open up to us other ways of seeing things.

Third, the word 'faithful' also carries a sense of desiring to honour what has gone before and remain in continuity with it. People who are described as faithful are those who hold on to what is valuable, even if holding on is costly, and who seek to live in a way that embodies the truths they prize highly. Nelson Mandela is universally admired for holding on to his belief that apartheid was wrong through his long years in prison and, at the same time, preserving his human dignity and generous nature. He remained faithful to his core convictions about human beings. That doesn't mean that such beliefs are held in air-tight boxes or locked safes, always taking the same form and never changing. Being faithful is more demanding than that. After his release Nelson Mandela, who because of his beliefs opposed apartheid by public protest and because of his beliefs kept faith while in prison, had to find a way to express the same values in the new South Africa when the country was seeking to recover from violence, brutality, bloodshed and destruction. This he did with others in enacting the Truth and Reconciliation Commission to bring truth, forgiveness and new possibilities for victims and perpetrators alike. He continued to be faithful but by doing very different things. Thus, faithful reflection is not to preserve everything of the past but to identify how we can live in continuity with the faith of our forebears but in an appropriate way for our age.

In this way then faithful reflection is reflection that is undertaken by people of faith, using the historic resources of the faith, for the purpose of living faithfully in the present. Robert Kinast coined the phrase 'making faith sense' for the same way of approaching life from the perspective of Christian faith. This is an attractive term, which you may prefer. For the reasons set out above and because there is much written on reflection that will help us understand the idea, we will use faithful reflection in this chapter.

A deeper look at reflection

People have been writing about reflection since the early part of the twentieth century. The influential educational thinker, John Dewey, spoke of it as a form of thinking with a specific purpose or intention, that is, thinking to achieve an end or to solve a problem.

The idea was given a high profile by the work of Donald Schön.[6] Schön saw the term 'reflection' as best able to describe

---

6 Donald Schön, *The Reflective Practitioner*, London: Temple Smith,

the type of learning that operates in the hectic world of business managers and professional workers. He suggested that people in these roles did much of their most important learning in their jobs, as they reflected on their decisions and actions and their consequences. By paying careful attention to what happens in practice they are able to improve and develop their perform-ance and extend appropriate and useful knowledge. They were in effect reflective practitioners. This established some other features of reflection. First, it suggested that reflection was a natural human process that was particularly suited to ongo-ing learning. Indeed, reflection becomes more important as we become more experienced and accumulate much knowledge. Second, it is a way of learning that works well in a fast-changing environment, enabling people to adapt quickly and effectively to new challenges. Third, reflection was particularly helpful in relation to refining ideas that inform practical actions. It seems to loop back and forward, from practice to theory, to practice, in an interactive way that hones ideas and improves their reali-zation. Although, like Dewey, Schön thought that reflection was important in problem solving, it was, he argues a much more subtle and versatile thinking facility for ongoing develop-ment and lifelong learning. His publications and work have exerted considerable influence on the training of professionals from doctors, nurses and managers to police, sales executives and night club bouncers ever since.

Jennifer Moon, in a wide ranging survey of literature on reflection,[7] came to the conclusion that reflection is a 'relatively simple mental activity' which works particularly on the inte-gration of new knowledge, structuring things we already know into some sort of framework or refining how we view things. It is often prompted into action by encounters with unfamiliar

1983; Donald A. Schön, *Educating the Reflective Practitioner: Toward a New Design for Teaching and Learning in the Professions*, The Jossey-Bass Higher Education Series, San Francisco: Jossey-Bass, 1987.

7 Jennifer A. Moon, *Reflection in Learning and Professional Devel-opment*, London: Kogan Page, 1999.

knowledge or experience, by problems that have to be solved or tasks that have to be completed.

Reflection and Learning

Moon sets her understanding within a view of the nature of learning which involves five stages or levels of learning.

1 *Noticing* is the first level. We notice something when it comes into view through our senses. We see a scene for the first time, we hear music on the radio, we catch a scent as we pass a garden or a factory, or we encounter some ideas in the newspaper or a book. We are for a moment aware of this new knowledge but that may be the end of the experience. It may be lodged in the memory in some form but is quickly forgotten, at least until our memory is prompted by a similar sight or smell or noise. The reason for this forgetting is that we do not attach significance to it and we do not want or need to carry this knowledge with us. Of course, there are those people who are very skilled at remembering these random bits of information and they are particularly good folk to have on your team at a trivia quiz, but for most of us, our memories are not that good and the information slips away. Of course, what we notice may be determined to some extent by what we are attuned to already, what we are interested in and how we view the world. In this way our noticing may be filtered but it is not ultimately limited by this filter. New things can and do come to our attention.

2 *Making sense* is the next stage. Having noticed some new thing, we may be interested enough to remember what we noticed. We may attach words to it by thinking a sentence or two, such as, 'I like that view, it is beautiful. I especially like the colour and shape of the trees along this river bank at this autumn time.' We may tell someone about the incident at work as a story and in so doing provide a structure and sense to it. We are much more likely to remember this – when you have told one person, it is easy to tell another because you

now have a sensible way of narrating the event. Equally, we may have been interested in a new idea and can explain it, as least roughly, to a friend. These things have more significance for us but are still, however, only loosely connected to our existing knowledge. Over time these too are likely to fade in our minds.

3 *Making meaning* is the stage when learning is assimilated into our view of the world. The knowledge has a deeper significance for us because it is connected to how we do our job, or how we see family life or what we think are the important values to live by. We make the new knowledge part of our long-term bank of knowledge by linking it in a meaningful way with the knowledge we already have. It is possible through this that some of the ideas we already hold may be modified as we relate the new material to what we previously know but, in the main, the new knowledge fits with what we know already.

4 *Working with meaning* is where there is no need for continued contact with original sources and the ordering and meaning given is influenced by the ideas accumulating from ongoing learning. In other words, over time we may change how we view and think about things, because our brains make connections, gather various bits of knowledge into related clusters or frame some of our ideas together to make a picture. You may well have said to someone, 'I used to think of such and such like this but now I think it better to view it in a different way.' If you have, you have been giving a new meaning to the knowledge you have. The knowledge has changed only inasmuch as you have given it new meaning. It is like changing the furniture around in your living room. After hours of shifting chairs, sofas, TVs, coffee tables, lamps and pictures, the room looks completely different but the same furniture is in the room. What has changed is the relationship of the items to each other and to the features of the room in which they are held. By rearranging and reordering our knowledge we give it different meanings over time.

5 *Transforming meaning* is the highest level or stage of learning and refers to a major shift in our view of the world. A
conversion experience, be that from being an atheist to being
a Christian or from a Marxist to a liberal, would be a good
example of transforming meaning. It is as if many of the
pieces that make up our world view and our view of ourselves
are dismantled and put back together in an entirely new way.
This is not so much moving the furniture around in a room
but rebuilding a house. The building bricks are the same but
the bungalow is changed into a tall three-storey townhouse.
We have changed the frame as well as the relationship of the
elements inside it. The change may be prompted by an incident or crisis but it is unlikely to be caused entirely by such
an instance. It is more likely that the accumulation of shifts
of meaning operating within us over some time is such that
only a major transformation of meaning will enable us to
hold it together meaningfully.

In this view of the nature of learning, reflection is not the
whole of learning. In the first two levels, *noticing* and *making
sense*, reflection is the not the leading factor and may not be
operating at all. Reflection is, however, a widespread, common feature. Most people have the capacity to reflect and do
so often, either consciously or unconsciously. It appears to be
most at work in stages 3, 4 and 5 when we are making, developing or transforming meaning. So reflection has something
to do with making meaningful sense of things, often things we
already know, and ordering the knowledge we hold within us.

Moon makes two other important points about reflection.
First she is careful not to identify reflection too closely with a
purely cognitive activity. She sees it as a type of thinking but
does not by this mean that is simply an intellectual activity or
reserved for the intelligent. Learning is not to be equated with
head knowledge, neither is knowledge meant to be restricted to
standard school subjects. Reflection relates to all forms of our
knowledge: thinking (cognitive), feeling (affective) and doing
(psycho-motor). What is more, it is clear from Schön's work

that reflection works very effectively in the development of skills, attitudes and emotions.

Second, she argues that emotion has a part to play in reflection. According to Moon, there are three possible ways of conceiving the role of emotion in reflection. First, emotion could be a part of the process.[8] That is, it actively contributes to the way in which a person is reflecting and to the outcome of the process. She notes Emil Bruner's observation that, in the search for a memory of something, it is often a feeling about the content of the memory that reaches consciousness first. Second, emotion could be the content or focus for reflection, as it often is in counselling. Third, emotion may direct or steer the process of reflection so that it is not under immediate voluntary control. The place of emotion in reflection is supported by others. O'Connell Killen and de Beer, for example, emphasize the importance of feelings in the search for meaning and suggest a link between feelings and metaphors for both the understanding of meaning and for the breakthrough into new insight.[9] Daniel Goleman gives strong support to this from his argument for the primacy of the emotions in the brain.[10] The research work on the area of the brain called the amygdala, concerned with the emotions, indicates that not only does it play a powerful role in acquiring, developing and controlling emotional responses, it also acts as a router for sending messages to all parts of the brain and is linked with mental structuring and ordering.[11] Hence many of our deepest ideas have an emotional component.

---

8 There appears to be a typographical error at this point in Moon's text. The relevant sentence in the section dealing with emotion (p. 95 para 2, sentence three) reads 'Reflection could be a part of the process of reflection'. It seems clear from the next two sentences that she intended the word 'Emotion' to be the first word in this sentence.

9 Patricia O'Connell Killen and John de Beer, *The Art of Theological Reflection*, New York: Crossroad, 1995.

10 D. Goleman, *Emotional Intelligence: Why it Can Matter more than IQ*, London: Bloomsbury, 1996.

11 Alistair Smith, 'What the most recent brain research tells us about learning' in Frank Banks and Ann Shelton Mayes (eds), *Early Professional Development for Teachers*, London: Open University & David Fulton, 2001, pp. 106–32.

Implicit in what Moon says is the importance of the relationship between reflection and personal integrity or the sense of self. What we believe about the world and what we believe about ourselves are deeply connected and a change in one will affect the other.

All these aspects of reflection are involved in faithful reflection. In faithful reflection we are seeking to make meaningful sense of new information, working on how it relates to ideas and knowledge we already hold; reviewing and ordering our knowledge over time and changing circumstances; allowing our emotions and our behaviour as well as our thoughts to be considered together and in relation to each other; and being concerned about who we are and how we live with integrity. The main difference between faithful reflection and other forms of reflection is that we engage in this as people of faith; we self-consciously use the resources of our faith to help our reflecting and our aim is always to be better, more faithful followers of Christ.

Robert Kinast using his term 'making faith sense' puts it like this:

Making faith-sense means fitting one's life into the pattern of faith values, beliefs, and ideals that have been handed on from previous generations. However, 'fitting in' does not mean slavish conformity to the past or rationalising your actions artificially. It means creating a personal, practical way of living, consistent with a faith view of life.[12]

Faithful reflection in action: Some examples

Moira is a primary school teacher of some 20 years' experience. She has made steady progress in her career and is well respected by colleagues. Indeed she is recognized as a high-quality teacher with whom students are often placed on teaching practice. As a Christian, she has always seen her teaching as a way of

---

12 Robert L. Kinast, *Making Faith-Sense: Theological Reflection in Everyday Life*, Collegeville, MN: The Liturgical Press, 1999, p. 3.

serving others and helping give children a good start in life. Over the years, successive governments have wanted to raise standards of education and she has been involved in several new developments in the school with some energy and enthusiasm. Gradually but increasingly, however, she has felt caught between the demands of league tables and the pressure of the system on her to achieve results in her school on the one hand, and her own professional intuition about individual children's readiness for particular developments and activities, on the other. She felt that some children were forced too quickly into new learning, for which they were not ready, or at the expense of other parts of their growth and development by the need for the school to perform well in tests. It came to a head over one child in particular who she felt was struggling to keep up at the pace being set and to whom she was giving much time. The head who had listened to her concerns suggested that the child might be better in another school and then all the other children would benefit from her teaching skills. This caused Moira to consider whether she would be better in another school or not in teaching at all. It was while she was on a church weekend away that Moira found a little time to reflect. She talked to a friend for a couple of hours over the Saturday when the two of them were lagging behind on the afternoon walk. Her friend listened and encouraged her to talk further about it. The theme of the weekend was Christ's human life or, to give its theological title, the incarnation. One of the sessions had been about how Jesus worked within the given limitations of his particular given situation: he did not rid the land of the Roman occupation, he accepted the Temple was good but in some ways corrupt and he knew it was not possible to fulfil people's expectations of him. Yet in all these givens, he was able to live out God's love and care – healing the sick, challenging the powerful and giving people a taste of the coming kingdom of God. He was willing to work within but not be determined by the limitations of the world. Over the next few weeks, Moira began to make a connection between this idea of incarnation and her own circumstances. Perhaps, she thought, she could stay in teaching but work creatively and find ways forward. Instead of seeing her calling simply in terms of serving others, she began to see herself as having to find ways of including and developing those whom the system tended to marginalize. When the special needs responsibility was discussed in the school, some months later, she applied for it and began to work with all the staff on how to develop and deliver better programmes for all according to their particular needs. Reflection on her experience did not remove the problem but she had derived an understanding that enabled her to continue to work within the tension.

Paul is in his 50s. He works in training for a large bank and travels around a lot. He is also one of the leaders of a new church, based in and around a series of homes in a North of England town. The church has been modestly successful at attracting young professionals into the church community, where evangelism has been largely through friendship and around shared meal tables. Several of the couples that have joined the community are cohabiting rather than married and although some have eventually married, some have not. Paul has felt uncomfortable about this, as he grew up with the view that sex before marriage was wrong and that Christians would get married before living together, but, on the other hand, he is glad that these young people have become committed to the way of Christ, and has kept his reservations to himself. Then his daughter, who has recently left university and started a job, tells him she is going to move in with her boyfriend. Paul is faced with both how to respond immediately and with longer term issues. When his daughter and boyfriend next come to stay does he offer them a shared double bed or single beds in separate rooms? He does not want to spoil the relationship with his daughter. He decides that it is something that he must investigate and reflect on. He reads the statistics and some of the explanations for why people cohabit rather than marry and he recognizes that a wedding service doesn't guarantee long-term commitment. Most important in his research he discovers wedding services to mark the beginning of married life are a relatively recent development, dating from the sixteenth century in Britain. Some cultures use a wedding service to celebrate a marriage years after the couple have set up home together. What is more significant is that Paul has up until now assumed that a wedding ceremony followed by lifelong marriage was the norm in the Bible. On examination, he finds that there are several patterns of marriage relationship in the Bible, some of which are no longer followed, and there is very little about wedding ceremonies. Jesus attended a wedding celebration (John 4) but there are no details of when this occurred in the relationship of the couple and in any case the emphasis in John's story is about the new life that Jesus brings not how weddings customs are to be observed. The story in Genesis about Isaac and Rebecca seems to suggest that the marriage was made by the two of them moving into the same tent, and nothing else. He begins to think that perhaps while ceremonies may be good both to celebrate and make the marriage public, the heart of marriage seems to be something to do with commitment, love and long-term faithfulness.

Darren works for an advertising agency. The firm is very competitive but also keen to be sensitive to the needs of consumers, so they can retain contracts and attract new clients. For this reason, the agency was one of the first to have its executives take a racism awareness programme, to use focus groups and to listen to feminist and other critiques of advertising stereotypes and images. Darren is pleased to work for such a receptive company. Recently, he has been part of small group making radio adverts for a charity that is concerned with disability. It has been a very creative and thought-provoking piece of work. The team were involved not simply by talking with people running the charity but also in talking with disabled people on how they felt in a variety of circumstances. They did some survey work on how 'non-disabled' perceive those with disability. In the end, they went for a series of short stories and reflections spoken by people with different forms of disability or impairment, with a short punch line challenging people to think again on how they thought about and related to those with disability. Darren has been very challenged by the experience. It has made him acutely aware of the language he uses – he no longer uses the term handicapped, and he is careful to talk about *people* with impairment or disability rather than use terms like 'the disabled', which somehow seem to push people further away in the mind. He was most moved talking to a very able women, a councillor active in local politics, who was dependent on an electric wheelchair for mobility. On her visits to London she would regularly wait in the street for up to an hour trying to hail a taxi, while being passed by dozens of empty cabs. She, though remarkable in her work and achievements for others, was often deliberately passed by because the sight of her wheelchair caused taxi drivers to avoid her, despite the fact that regulations require ramp facilities in London taxis. This has made Darren think about how inclusive his church is and is now sharply aware of the sloppy way images and language are used in church. Recently, in his cell group people were asked to say how they picture God, and Darren found himself saying 'God is in a wheelchair, unable to move much, loving us, wanting relationship and waiting for us join in to build a better world.'

Let us look at reflection through these experiences and draw out some aspects of the practice.

1 Reflection is prompted naturally out of life experience

Moira knew she was at a crisis point in her career and was looking for an opportunity to work through it. The need for reflection was provoked by her growing discontent with her teaching experience. Her friend was fortunately at hand and gave Moira the chance to reflect. The weekend theme supplied some theological resource material for her to develop a new understanding of her calling. Paul's need for reflection came out of a discomfort in his church life and the critical incident of his daughter's announcement. In Darren's case, new encounters and experiences came his way through his work, which made him reflect on his own behaviour, his church's life and his ideas of God. No one else had to engineer these learning opportunities. They were all life based and stimulated out of the daily worlds of these three Christian disciples.

Sometimes people are aware that things are not right or that there are issues to think about but are not sure exactly what they are. Kinast suggests two good gauges to watch. One is our emotions, the other is our conversation. When we feel frustration, anger, sadness or general unsettledness these emotions may be good indicators of the value, importance, and meaning of things that are happening in your life. Likewise, when something is bothering us, or exciting us, we talk about it often and sometimes in unexpected situations. If you can stand back and ask yourself what it is that you find yourself talking about a lot, you may identify something that requires some reflection time.

Reflection can be intentionally prompted or enabled, through the provision of space and opportunity. This was in part offered by the weekend for Moira and the cell group for Darren. A spiritual director or soul friend can help us by giving time for this purpose. Likewise, a mutual support or covenanted group can serve the same role. Special events in the learning life of the church can be organized. We will look at some of these later in the book. These provide the opportunities and structures for reflecting, however. They do not create the source or focus of the reflection. Rather they work with issues that arise out of the everyday life of these dispersed disciples.

2 Reflection needs time and resource

While the need for reflection arises naturally and the ability to reflect seems to be universal among human beings, it does need both time and resource to work well. People often find that they are too busy or events happen so quickly that their life is moved on without any opportunity to reflect. It can be months or years after something significant that people have the time to think about it from a faith perspective. Even then they may not immediately be able to make sense of it or find a way forward because they have not yet located the resources they need to make meaningful sense of their experience. The church weekend away, the cell group, and the Christian friend were all important resources for Moira and Darren. For Paul, the opportunity to study and research was helpful too. In his work on marriage and cohabitation he discovered some surprising things that became useful in constructing his new or rather modified view of marriage. Moira too found some theological resources in the church weekend that connected with her search for meaning and this gave her ideas to work with. The resources we need include both other people and truths from our faith in scriptures and the tradition of the Church.

Tradition here is a positive word. It refers to the rich treasure house of stories, writing, hymns, poetry, arts and music that Christians have lived, created and passed on to us and which are still carrying that life as they connect with our life and situation. Discovering these can be life-giving in that it can open up for us fresh, new possibilities. It is like someone making a quilt and getting to the point where the material will run out but then finding in a cupboard lots of new material that had been put away for exactly this purpose. The discovery may not only allow one to complete the work but it may add new patterns and colours to the crafting.

New information may not be necessary. We may already know the story or be familiar with the text. It is simply that it suddenly comes alive in a new and different way. The church weekend was not the first time Moira had thought about the incarnation, but there was something in the way it was presented this time that connected for her and transformed both the concept and what it meant in her life.

3 Reflection works through fact and imagination

If you have ever encountered the phenomenon of *Godly Play*[13] you will know the special way stories are told within it. They usually involve a box of carved wooden figures and simple

---

13 Jerome Berryman, *Godly Play*, Minneapolis: Augsburg Fortress, 1995; Jerome Berryman *Teaching Godly Play*, Nashville: Abingdon 1995. See also www.godlyplay.org.uk

artefacts or objects, such as a piece of cloth for a road or a shape for a building. As the storyteller carefully and slowly lifts out the figures and objects, the listeners (children and adults) are invited into a very familiar and simply told story, usually from the Bible. There is an air of expectancy around the event of the storytelling. What is striking, however, is how short and plain the narrative is, and yet it is infused with possibility, often marked by the storyteller posing 'I wonder' questions during the story and especially at the end: 'I wonder where the man would go next?' 'I wonder what he would say to his family?' 'I wonder which was your favourite part of the story?' The effect of the 'I wonder' questions is to encourage the listeners' imaginations to be active, taking them into the story and allowing the story to relate to their experiences and life. After the story, listeners may choose to play themselves with the figures to retell the story or tell the story in another way, or they may paint or write or do other work that allows their imaginations to take their ideas further.

Godly play represents an extraordinary bringing together of Bible and imagination. Faithful reflection works in a similar way. On the one hand, it concerns itself with real-life situations and issues that are often best explored by a simple honest telling of the story, incident or event. With honesty and simplicity it is possible to get closer to the key issues and concerns. Yet it is also about being open to new ways of seeing and understanding those accounts and responding to them. Notice that Darren told his cell group that God was in a wheelchair. This imagining of God was not of a helpless person but rather a person of dignity and strength and yet without power to force others to do what was needed but who made an appeal and offered an invitation to join in making a new and better world. Of course, the picture was like the person he met through his work, but it also caught something about the open vulnerability of God expressed on the cross and felt in the missionary experience of Paul (1 Corinthians 1.18ff. and 2 Corinthians 4). The picture was the result of imagination, which captured and combined experience and truth in a way that disclosed the deeper meaning of both. In a similar way, it was a leap of imagination for Moira to see herself within the framework of the incarnation as working with but not being determined by the situation.

Imagination is involved in reflection in the same way as an artist sees and creates familiar things in a fresh and different way. It connects and holds elements together so that we can make a new picture in which the individual facets relate together within a coherent whole.

4   Reflection works through words and images

Much of our thinking, speaking and making sense of life is done through words. Indeed, what I am doing at this moment in writing is setting words in some sort of order to convey my convictions and ideas. My success in communication depends to a large extent on my ability to find the right words and put them together in a way that makes sense to you the reader. Reflection, whether spoken, written or simply thought through in the mind is often through words in sentences, in half sentences or strings of words that express our feelings, thoughts and resolutions. O'Connor Killen and de Beer, in their work on theological reflection, argue that images are often a more important key to unlocking our meaning-making faculties. Their route to helping people to make faith sense of their lives is to encourage people to give particular attention to feelings. Thus if, for example, you are relating a story that has significance for you, as Moira did in talking to her friend, then they would suggest that you attend to the feelings that are evoked and stay with them for a time. You may find that images come to mind or if you try to give voice to your feelings in the language of imagery, a particular picture fits well. An image here appears to be a word picture or metaphor, which incorporates both affective and cognitive perceptions of our experience. They possess a strong ability to hold the emotional and rational dimensions of our human perception and can work as a sort of shorthand or code for storing and recalling our complex knowledge. 'Images symbolise our experience. They capture the totality of our felt response to reality in a given situation.'[14] All this fits well with the work of Goleman and Moon, referred to above, and also with studies of the way individuals work in professions where large quantities of information and experience are held through an intuitive association with images or metaphors.[15] It also coheres with the use of imagination in reflection.

In practical terms, it means that images may play a key role in the way we see and respond to things, and thus exploring images, pictures and metaphors is likely to facilitate reflection. In my early years of working with people, I came up with the idea of using photographs and images to start people talking about their faith. Sometimes these were explicitly religious pictures, often they were not obviously faith related but simply photos taken of everyday life. I never ceased to be amazed how much people would see in these pictures and how quickly it got people into discussing the deep things of their faith. These images often connected into and sparked with pictures they were carrying within them which were brought into play in their sharing.

O'Connor Killen argues that the attention to images, especially ones that are no longer helping us, sometimes allows other images to emerge and replace them in our mind – images that make more sense and release purpose and energy in us for our living. You might like to consider how images operated in the people at the heart of the three stories above.

5 Reflection involves thinking and action
In all three stories changes in thinking led to changes in behaviour. Moira not only changed her view of her role as a teacher but this led to a changed way of working, through volunteering to be the special needs co-ordinator and supporting other staff. Darren began to change the way he spoke about disability,

---

14 O'Connell Killen and de Beer, *The Art of Theological Reflection*, p. 37.

15 See Michael Eraut, *Developing Professional Knowledge and Competence*, London and Washington: Falmer, 1994.

realizing that the way he spoke affected the way he and others thought and acted. Paul's action is not outlined in the story but it becomes apparent in the way he responded to the implicit questions of what he should do when his daughter and boy-friend came to visit – he offered them a double-bedded room. What is more, his research and study led him to talk with other church leaders about the issue and to their church starting a series of workshops about relationships, which was aimed at helping people explore issues of commitment and sexuality.

Of course, the stories might have gone a different way. Moira might have had a breakdown, left the school or changed careers; Paul might have taken a stand against his daughter's view and Darren might have kept his work life quite separate and distinct from his personal and church life. Without the change of thinking, their action might have been quite differ-ent. Perhaps because all three discovered the need for reflection in a practical issue that called for a response or decision, their reflection was translated in action quickly in the very place that the issue arose.

It is not always so. Sometimes there is a gap between our reflecting and our acting. As the old adage goes, 'When all is said and done, more is said than done!' Kinast offers us some reasons why turning our reflection into action can be difficult. He sees obstacles which may need to be faced. In the first place, when we begin with an insight or conviction arrived at through reflection we are functioning in a different way from when we take action. It may take time and thought to see what new action is consistent with our new thinking and how to enact it. What is more, our habits and instincts are deep-rooted. They have been built up over many years so that we can act without thinking in lots of everyday situations. Changes of action will need to confront and change habits. Another reason we stall is that we may not feel comfortable with practical implications when we have worked them out. People may not have reacted positively to Darren's new-found care over language about dis-ability. They may feel an implied criticism or see him as pedantic or simply following the trendy 'PC' groups. Darren may feel that on some occasions he needs to challenge not only language but also practical arrangements and assumptions made in his church community about people with disability. He may not relish the reactions he may provoke. Finally, Kinast argues, we may not have the resources to, or be in a position to implement what we want to do, in that change may involve others and levels of power we don't have. All this makes the gap between reflecting and acting hard to cross but with planning all but the last obstacle can be overcome and even finding resources and influencing structures can become a strategic aim.

There is another point to be made here too. Sometimes a change in our actions comes from a change in our thinking, and sometimes a change in our thinking comes from a change in our actions. Darren's story represents some changes in his work and contacts that provoked a challenge to his thinking. To go on working with disabled people perhaps he would need to change his thinking and speaking. In this sense he was in part acting himself into a new way of thinking as well as thinking himself into a new way of acting. I remember a student minister on placement in an asylum seekers' and refugees' support centre, sharing how she had gone with all sorts of preconceptions, which after three months' work had completed changed. Doing the work made her change her ideas. For many of us, the change in thinking and the change in action will be a to-ing and fro-ing between our thoughts and acts as we work out what our reflection means for us and our lives.

6   Reflection is on situations and self

The final point to note from the examples is that although reflection was in each case about an issue or problem, the reflection involved a subjective dimension. The person doing the reflecting was, in each case, thinking about who she (or he) was and what views to hold as a Christian in this situation. In each case, self-perception was a part of the reflection. Paul, for example, has to consider where his view of marriage came from alongside the situation he was meeting and the research he then undertook. His ideas about marriage came from his own parents and church background. He had absorbed these views and saw them as part and parcel of a Christian view of the world and a big part of his own identity as a Christian. The self that does the reflecting has itself been shaped in the past and carries much of that history into any new reflection undertaken. It will exert a strong influence on how we do our reflecting and the outcomes in daily living. Thus, it is important to encourage in any reflection some exploration of my own reflecting. Why do I think, feel and react in the way that I am doing? What factors are at work in me and how is this influencing the reflection? These are not easy questions to answer, for some of our history is hidden from us in the past or too close to us for us to be able to see it clearly. This does not mean it is impossible or doomed to be determined by forces we cannot control. We can sometimes see why we react as we do and what other elements might be at work when we are reflecting on issues and concerns, and we may see better still as we practise. To ignore this dimension its the real danger, for not only does it make us less able to reflect effectively but it closes us to the healing and forgiveness and shaping of our spirit by the Spirit of God at work in us.

The technical word for an awareness of the self in the process of reflection is reflexivity and it is often applied not simply to individuals but also to groups and cultures and particular histories. It is the case that to be black or white, to be male or female, to have grown up in poverty or wealth, significantly shapes how we see ourselves and influences how we engage with life. These are not simply our personal histories, they are part of larger histories, which often go back long before our birth. Antony Reddie's action-research on Christian education for young Afro-Caribbean disciples is important here for it demonstrates the critical value of taking one's ethnic history, culture and language into the process of learning and reflecting.[16]

16 Anthony Reddie, *Nobodies to Somebodies: A Practical Theology for Education and Liberation*, Peterborough: Epworth Press, 2003.

Nurturing reflective habits

So, if faithful reflection is a core discipline of discipleship, how do we get better at it, how do we nurture it in ourselves and others and what can the Church do in its structures and learning activities to equip disciples to be faithful reflectors? In the final chapter we shall turn to the role of the gathered Church in preparing and supporting people as reflective disciples. Here we identify ways of nurturing the underlying skills and attitudes that help to develop a reflective faith approach to life.

Some exercises

When I had trouble with my back about ten years ago, I eventually saw a physiotherapist. She looked at my lifestyle – a lot of time sitting at a desk, working on a computer, a fair amount of time standing in a class room, in a pulpit or leading a worship congregation, and quite a lot of time driving. When I came to do some sport or tackled jobs in the garden, it was not surprising, she thought, that my back and neck were prone to give me trouble. She outlined a series of six exercises to do each morning to loosen up and stretch my back and neck and to ensure that they were supple and ready for other slightly more demanding tasks. It was one of the great miracle cures! I worked hard at first to do the exercises, and to get them firmly established in my morning routine and then they became part of daily life. I still do them most days and I have not so far had any further problems of this type.

It seems that the trick was to do little, often and to stretch in all the different ways that backs and necks are meant to but which were not much of a feature in my lifestyle.

In terms of discipleship, these are basic exercises for nurturing faithful reflection.

Practise attentiveness

In Luke 2.19 there is a short but evocative comment about Mary. Luke says 'Mary kept all these things, pondering them in her heart.' This comes after the birth of Jesus and the arrival of some very excited shepherds, and at the end of a long Lukan narrative that includes the Angel's words to Mary, the extraordinary happening with Mary's cousin Elizabeth and her husband Zechariah and the unprecedented census, which entails a long journey to Bethlehem. Almost the same words are used again after Mary and Joseph find Jesus in the Temple talking with the teachers of the law: 'his mother kept these things in her heart' (Luke 2.51). The verbs Luke uses, which we translate 'kept' (*sunetērei* and *dietērei*), can mean 'held', 'protected' or 'treasured'. It seems that these life events were kept in focus, held tenderly, given careful attention as a way of beginning to find their meaning.

In a post-modern image-filled and fast-moving world, attention spans are shortening. Practising attentiveness is vital if we are to penetrate beyond surface meanings. You can do this in any number of ways and with a multitude of types of focus. If you watch films at the cinema or DVDs, soap operas on TV or performances on stage, you can sharpen your attention skills by thinking about one character, and trying to see how the world looks or feels from that person's perspective. Ask yourself questions about what was going on in the plot. Look at the clothes and body language and the setting. What are they telling you about how the directors see what is happening? Some of the best documentaries on TV now are currently about particular life experiences, following people as they cope with an illness or compete in an international competition. While, of course, you are shown the story through someone else's eyes, the ability of these film-makers to give careful attention to the detail of individual stories is inspiring.

Attentiveness can be nurtured through simple observation of what goes on around us at home or in family or at work. Keeping a notebook or journal is a simple and effective way of holding something still, to see what is there. But it need not be so formally planned. The very ordinary mealtime stories that different members of the family tell of the events of their day can be opportunities for attentiveness and there is almost always more to be known by encouraging others to tell you more about an incident or experience.

All these ways of practising attentiveness are like pressing the pause button on the DVD or video player and looking at a still picture frozen on the screen. What you had not noticed in the background is now more obvious, the emotion of the key character is amplified or the absence of the accompanying music gives a different feel to the story. Some things are able to stand out because others are held still, if only for a moment.

Practise making connections

In Luke's verse about Mary (Luke 2.19) there is another interesting word. The Greek word which is translated as 'pondering' is made up of two words combined in one, one meaning 'together', and the other meaning 'to put or place or throw' (*sumballō*). So pondering suggests putting things together, holding them near to each other, even forcing them to be in relationship (the sense of 'throwing' together) to see what they mean. Luke is saying that Mary not only kept careful hold of the events but that she actively explored how they related to each other in order to make sense of them.

This kind of juxtaposing of one thing with another is a part of reflection. In faithful reflection it is to do with setting the scriptures and the tradition alongside one's life events and allowing them to speak to each other. Sometimes these things stand immediately next to each other, as with Mary's extraordinary and odd life events, and the challenge is to spot the connection and work out the meaning. At other times, we need to be active in making a link ourselves. You can practise this very simply by beginning with an incident or issue and asking 'What does this remind me of in the Bible?' or 'What stories come to mind when I think about this?' Alternatively, you can ask of a Bible reading you heard or read: 'To what in my life does this relate at the moment?' It need not be a Bible text or story that helps you make a connection. It could be a painting or a verse of a hymn that brings some insight. This doesn't mean that the first thing you think will be the best way to connect the two or of making meaning. Indeed, you can decide that the story or verse or picture that came to mind doesn't really parallel your life event or speak to it – though it is always worth staying with the things that come to mind for a little time. It may, however, allow you to begin a search for a better and more illuminating example. Again, making a note or telling a friend will strengthen your reflection.

Making good connections will also depend on expanding your knowledge of the scriptures and tradition. This means actively growing in your familiarity with the Christian faith in all its forms, through reading, study groups or events, watching documentaries and programmes or searching the internet for knowledge of the Bible and Christian history, theology, art, symbolism and architecture. As you learn more, you may well find yourself making connections and the more this grows, the richer the resource you will have to draw on.

Practise partnered conversations

Interestingly, the other use of the word translated 'pondering' (*sumballō*) in much of the New Testament is to do with encounter and conversation (Luke 14.31; Acts 14.15; Acts 17.18; 18.27; 20.14). Another way of putting things together is through conferring with others. This need not be simply with one person, it could be a group, or it could be different people on different occasions. However, the kind of trust and honesty and shared commitment to make meaning is often only built over a period of time. I think that the growth in the use of spiritual directors, prayer guides or soul friends is indicative of the need that many people feel for someone with whom they can share honestly about their faith journey and talk freely about God. Because talk about God is pushed to the private and personal sphere, even many Christians have become hesitant about using the language, as we noted earlier, but like the Israelites who spoke Hebrew behind the wall,[17] we need to practise faith language or else we will forget how to use it.

Partnered conversations are opportunities to rehearse connections you may have made and develop attentiveness with others. Focusing for a time on your partner or on another group member's story or concerns, and supporting them in finding meaning and direction can develop both skills. Making time for partnered conversations, either on a regular or occasional basis is a significant help to reflection. If you have not done this before, it may be valuable to have a set starting point, not unlike the early Methodist class meeting where set questions prompted the conversation and sharing. Asking someone, 'Where has God been in your experience recently?' or being asked 'What things in your life are most stretching your faith?' can give permission for yourself and others to speak about God. Conversations don't always have to be about your experience or problems in a narrow sense. You may want to talk about a film that has helped you think about God or something you have read, a sermon you have heard, or a story from Christian history that you have recently met. The rule is to take time to talk about God.

Practise prayerful expression and practical enactment

Reflection without some kind of outcome is not really faithful reflection. It may not, however, always be an observable behaviour change or action that can be pinpointed or measured. Take, for example, when some reflection on experience leads to a confirmation rather than a change in one's beliefs. Behaviour and action are likely to continue to be the same as before, yet that doesn't mean something significant has not happened. Through reflection you have recognized a gospel truth and seen its expression in your own life. This is a precious discovery and something to celebrate. It will strengthen your faith and give

---

17 See the discussion in Chapter 4 on disciples as bilingual.

you greater confidence in the gospel. Such growth should be a reason for thanksgiving, which could be offered in prayer, or worship, through testimony or marked in some other way. I have watched people paint a prayerful picture, or craft a clay model, write a poem or light a candle to mark such discoveries. These are prayerful expressions and can be a regular part of the rhythm of reflective discipleship.

Prayerful expression is no substitute for taking action, however. This too needs to be practised as part of a life that is changing to become more Christ-like. Saying sorry, changing one's attitudes, language and behaviour in line with one's reflection need not necessarily be big changes. Small alterations and initiatives can be effective and cumulative. When you have a new insight you should ask yourself: What small change would begin to express this in my home or work or church?

Practise personal accountability

The monastic orders and the early Methodists had one major thing in common. They practised accounting for the daily lives to one another. Not only did this involve being willing to tell honestly of their successes and failures, but they also agreed to the idea that others would tell them when they felt they were not living their Christian life as well as they might. 'Do you desire to be told your faults and that right plain?' was the question you were asked if you joined the Methodist band meetings. And you could be sure that if you signed up to this or the rules of Benedict, at some point someone would do just that! The reason for this hard truth-telling in John Wesley's mind was the self-deceit that all human being seem to share (Jeremiah 17.9). We need others to check that we are not deceiving ourselves. Such personal accountability with others is not easy to undertake and depends on a close-knit, supportive and loving group of people. Speaking the truth, as you see it, about someone else risks getting it very wrong and causing hurt and damage because we are not familiar with the details of other people's lives and circumstances. Perhaps this is even more the case in our mobile and post-modern society when we only see a small part of other people's story and situation.

For this reason we need to be more proactive about finding relationships in which we are committed to honesty and are willing to account for ourselves and our Christian living. In the realm of reflection this kind of help is needed because of reflexivity – the key involvement of ourselves in the reflection process and the thus the need to have another's perspective on our work in faithful reflection. This may be part of a relationship involving partnered conversations with a Christian friend. In many ways it will work well if it is but some people find a relationship based less on friendship and more on caring objectivity better – for example, with a spiritual director who will listen and reflect back to you where the story doesn't fit with what you have shared before, who will identify where there seems to be unsettledness in your account and who will ask you about the commitment to change you made on some previous occasion. However you pursue this, you need to work with someone whose confidentiality is secure.

You can begin again in simple ways by seeking to be honest with God – telling it as it is when you pray and perhaps being willing to ask someone to pray for you in relation to some of the avenues you are taking.

Reflection in the rhythm

All these practices require practice. That is, they are expressions of our commitment to the life of discipleship but also the means by which we grow into the new life offered us in Christ. They do not represent a formula for success but a set of exercises to develop faithful reflection. Like the apprentice who attends to the routine jobs that foster basic skills, however repetitive, with the intention of learning habits that carry competence for demanding work, we who seek to nurture reflective habits are building towards a mature discipleship that equips us to stay close to God and know how best to serve.

This could sound very like an individual endeavour but it is not so. We do this with and for others who share the journey of faith. In other words, we are called into discipleship as the Church. Our next, and final, chapter turns to the Church and asks the question: What kind of Church helps us to become reflective disciples?

6

Christian Communities in which Disciples Grow

The calling of the Church to nurture disciples

The question posed by all that I have written so far is: What kind of Church supports and nurtures reflective disciples? The answer to this question may at first sight seem straightforward. In Chapters 4 and 5 we identified attitudes and practices that are central to living in the rhythm: namely courageous openness, careful accountability, conscientious immersion in the tradition, constant prayerfulness and faithful reflection. Implicit in much that was said about these facets of discipleship are directions for the Church.

If we are to nurture *courageous openness*, we need church communities that encourage friendliness and generous hospitality, outgoing attitudes and boundary-crossing, risk-taking, adventurous initiatives. Such churches will hear sermons on these themes, will treasure and tell stories of human contact and risk taking and will listen to those who seek to put these attitudes into practice in both their success and failure. They may also initiate acts of hospitality or outreach that connect to the new, different or perhaps marginalized members of the locality or wider world. A drop-in centre for asylum seekers, a fun and friendly parenting class for young single mums or a partnership link with a church in another part of the world may all provide opportunity to form friendships and find God's presence in others. A series of meeting with members of the local mosque or Hindu temple may also open new doors.

If we wish to support disciples who practise *careful account-ability*, we need churches that place a high value on testimony, that provide a safe space to be honest about our successes and failures in discipleship, and that offer structures for truthful sharing and discipleship checks. Such churches will have small groups, prayer partners or a mentoring system for these purposes. They will devise liturgies to express candidly to God in words their own failings. They will seek to be transparent in finance and leadership decisions and may develop a simple 'rule of life' for their members.

Likewise, churches that are to feed disciples, so that they are deeply aware of the scriptures and Christian tradition, will provide learning opportunities in a variety of different learning styles to allow people to enter, own and interpret the tradition. Thus, they will not only teach and preach but also enable disciples to engage actively in the process of critical appropriation and will listen to the ways in which disciples make faith sense of their daily experiences. Their worship will be alive to the feel as well as the content of the scriptures and their leaders will give time to finding resources from the tradition that can extend, enrich and excite worshippers. Disciples in such churches can become *immersed in the tradition*.

Constant prayerfulness will grow out of a church community that prays at every level of its life together. Such a church will introduce people to prayer and explore different ways of praying. It will pray on every occasion that its members come together. It will mix prayers from the tradition with extemporary praying and will offer ways of praying for beginners and those who need new patterns because life has altered in its shape and rhythm. It will stand with those who are finding it difficult to pray and bear them in its shared prayer life. It will create imaginative prayer spaces, temporary or more permanent. In its range of praying it will include praise, petition, honest frustration and lamenting grief and it will remember publicly and privately the everyday work lives of its members to share the burden of the dilemmas and challenges they face. It may make prayer boards or prayer books available to all its members and visitors and be disciplined in persisting with prayers requested. It will encourage all to be pray-ers and will support the development of those with a specific calling to prayer ministry. Above all, it will carry a sense that speaking to God and listening for God is at the heart of its life and work.

If we are to nurture *faithful reflection* in each other, we need to belong to churches that practise reflection in their gatherings and encourages reflection in our home, work and leisure lives. Such churches will actively prompt people to tell stories and share incidents from their everyday lives in order to seek and celebrate God's presence. They will set time and resource aside for quiet days and sharing days and study weekends. They will seek to stimulate and release imagination in their members by drawing on a wide range of images and metaphors, Christian art and members' insights. They will promote a Godly Play-style 'I wonder. . .' disposition in young and old. Disciples will regularly pose vocational questions for each other, such as: 'What do think God is saying to you or calling you to do?' and will try to discern the answer with people. As a community the church will set time aside to reflect together on events in its own life or wider community and consider together its meaning in faith terms and determine its action on the basis of theological convictions discerned through disciplined patterns of reflection and careful conferring.

In all these ways the church will seek to build a way of being church that embeds its key values in its gathered life and will devise activities and programmes that promote and nurture the attitudes and practices of reflective disciples.

An ideal church?

What I have sketched here represents the church I would like to belong to. It sounds vibrant, attractive and adventurous and it is rich in the initiatives and resources needed for twenty-first century followers of Jesus. But there are several problems in creating a vision of the Church this way. First, it looks too good to be true. Perhaps you know a church just like this or even belong to one, but for most people this is an aspirational dream. The Christian community to which they belong may have a few of these features but not all. For some, their church congregation is much more severely limited in time, resources, personnel and ideas. Survival and holding on to the world view by the fingernails is much closer to the experienced reality. This is not an argument for limiting the vision, however. Dreaming dreams and seeing visions is the stuff of the Spirit and the people of God. The picture needs to be large and the imagination charged, if we are going to fashion together a Church of disciples for today.

A second objection may be that the Christian community I have in mind depends too much on inherited church models. What form or forms the emerging church will take is by definition not yet known and it may be that the way I have framed the features and activities of the church for disciples sounds too much like the large, well-resourced, community with substantial premises and a sense of identity within a geographical location. Inevitably, I will envision out of what I know but I have sought here to identify characteristics before giving examples precisely for Christian readers to consider as new forms of church emerge. My picture has a missionary orientation and a discipleship interest that needs to be part of developing new ways of being church.

The third and final problem with this vision is perhaps the most serious. This picture of church appears to be driven by those who belong to it or those who wish to belong to it. Is it therefore consumerist, simply making a church to provide the things we followers want or think we need? While I don't accept this because the vision here grows out of a picture of God, as well as an analysis of the nature of discipleship and the problems and dilemmas of the early twenty-first century, I nevertheless recognize that it is not the only way to build a vision of the Church and that such an approach may risk missing some very important aspects of what it means to be the Church. By choosing to emphasize the needs of dispersed church disciples in the world, there is a danger of promoting the kind of individualism that already threatens the corporate calling of Christians. We must turn briefly then to other perspectives on the Church.

The calling of the Church to be a kingdom community[1]

The calling of Jesus to his first disciples was a calling to community. Once those men and women began to follow, they found themselves in a series of relationships not only with Jesus but with other followers in the travelling Jesus community. And it was in this set of relationships that they discovered much about what the realm of God meant. In this kingdom community, for example, there is no hierarchy and greatness is accorded to those who serve others, not to those who want power, as the group found out when James and John wanted to claim the powerful positions in the coming kingdom. It was while living together they discovered that the kingdom is not exclusive but open, as they learned when they tried to block children from coming to Jesus and as they accompanied Jesus into Pharisees' houses and demoniacs' dens. It was in community that Peter made his boast that he would never deny Jesus and had to face himself when his boast was proved vain. It was in this extraordinary community that prostitutes and tax collectors lived with zealots, fishermen and a woman connected with Herod's palace, all equally welcome. It was in and through the experience of this intimate society that Jesus taught his followers the reality of the kingdom of God.

In the Acts of the Apostles, it is significant that the Spirit comes upon the disciples when they are together in the upper room as a community. The action of the Spirit drives them out to proclaim the truth and significance of the resurrection but equally importantly it also reforms, expands and deepens the Christian community. The cameo pictures that Luke offers us in Acts 2.42–7 and Acts 4.33–5 are of an extraordinary community in which 'all who believed were together and had all things in common' who 'broke bread at home and ate their

---

1 See Chapter 1.

food with glad and generous hearts' and where 'there was not a needy person among them'. These pictures signal to us that the kingdom community was reborn and renewed as a vital part of the Christian message. They also witness to the importance of the community as a sign of God at work and as a place where disciples learn what it means to be followers of Jesus.

There are some things, it seems, that can only be learned by living in God's alternative society which is the gathered Church. Stanley Hauerwas speaks of the crucial role of the gathered and visible Church in forming disciples in his seminal book *Resident Aliens*. Borrowing categories from John Howard Yoder, he sees the best model of the Church as a confessing Church which:

> seeks to be the visible church, a place clearly visible to the world, in which people are faithful to their promises, love their enemies, tell the truth, honor the poor, suffer for righteousness, and thereby testify to the amazing community creating power of God.[2]

It is likely that for most followers the first experience or glimpse of the life of the kingdom will be in some form of Christian community and it is here over time that they learn to see the world in a different way. It is in and through this experience of being the body of Christ that we gradually are reshaped by the reality of God's gracious kingdom.

> Here is a community in which even small, ordinary occurrences every Sunday, like eating together in Eucharist, become opportunities to have our eyes opened to what God is up to in the world and to be part of what God is doing. If we get good enough at forgiving the strangers who gather around the Lord's Table, we hope that we shall get good at forgiving the strangers who gather with us around the breakfast table. Our everyday experience of life in the congregation

---

2 Stanley Hauerwas and William H. Willimon, *Resident Aliens*, Nashville: Abingdon Press, 1989, p. 40.

is training in the arts of forgiveness; it is everyday, practical confirmation of the truthfulness of the Christian vision.[3]

To see discipleship only in terms of personal individual actions is to miss the truth and to set ourselves up to fail. Hauerwas makes this clear by pointing to the Sermon on the Mount (Matthew 5). He rejects this as a set of high ethical instructions for the few – the 'heroic ethical superstars'. He also rejects the view that such ideals have to be modified when placed in the public political arena.[4] Rather, he sees this as an invitation to form a 'visible, practical Christian community'. If it were a set of instructions for well-intentioned individuals (even those who follow Jesus), it would not help. Its demands are extraordinary – to love enemies and persecutors, to be non-violent in all circumstances, to speak the truth and keep promises, to avoid promiscuity and to be faithful in marriage – and its perceptions are the polar opposite to the usual ways of seeing thing – that the poor are blessed and God is to be found among those who mourn and are reviled. Anyone seeking to live in this way in his or her own strength is doomed to fail.

> The Sermon on the Mount is not primarily addressed to individuals, because it is precisely as individuals that we are most apt to fail as Christians. Only through membership in non-violent community can violent individuals do better.[5]

These things can only be realized in a community of people committed to Jesus, in relationship with each other and infused by the Holy Spirit.

Thus, there is a primary calling to be a community. This is of the essence of discipleship. Community is not an optional extra. It is not advocated because it is better to be together than on our own. It is necessary because it is the place where the

---

3 Hauerwas and Willimon, *Resident Aliens*, p. 91.

4 As advocated by Reinhold Niebuhr according to Hauerwas and Willimon, *Resident Aliens*, p. 76.

5 Hauerwas and Willimon, *Resident Aliens*, p. 77.

truth of God's revelation is being lived, sometimes weakly and fallibly, often imperfectly but where God's Spirit continually breaks in and works through our weak humanity to manifest the truth. It is only by participating in this community that we begin to see the world as it is, now God has acted in Christ, and only through it that we are able to act on this reality.

Seeing God's reality is the key. For this reason a major part of the gathered Church's life is in worship. In worship we are busy 'looking in the right direction'.[6]

In my youth there was a popular worship song with the words:

Turn your eyes upon Jesus, look full in his wonderful face
And the things of earth will grow strangely dim in the light of his glory and grace.

Perhaps because it was for a time widely popular, its theology was occasionally debated. Some criticized the song because they said that coming to worship was not to let the things of the world grow dim. To do so was to indulge in escapism. We needed not to leave our daily lives behind but to bring them into worship, to offer them to God and to gain a better perspective on how to live with and respond to these realities. You would guess from what I have written in earlier chapters that I have some sympathies for this point of view. There is, however, another point of view. Namely, that the vision of reality conveyed in the Christian message is such a radically different one from the everyday 'normal' assumptions of how the world operates, that you have to keep revisiting it and allowing it to shape your viewing of everything else or else it will be squeezed out by the dominant ideology of the world ('the things of the earth'). These interpretations of reality grow dim because they are shown to be false when viewed in the light of God's revelation in Jesus. The only way to get a new perspective on these things is to re-acquaint yourself with the vision of the kingdom.

6 Hauerwas and Willimon, *Resident Aliens*, p. 95.

So our calling to follow Jesus is at the same time a calling to be a community of Christ, where in living together we discover the reality and rule of God, delight in it, seek to embody it, and encounter its liberating power in action. We do not gather simply to feed our daily discipleship needs but also to create and sustain and grow community and to glimpse again the true state of things. This is both a gift of the Spirit and our commitment and hard work. It requires the energies not only of leaders but of all God's gathered people.

A gathered Church will, as a primary aim, seek to focus on how things really are by looking towards God's character and purpose seen in Jesus. Its worship must point to and enact this reality and its community life must focus on its truth. Such a Church will be concerned with telling God's story, in every way possible: through word, song, music, art, drama and performance. It will seek ways of worship and shared life that enable people to practise its truth and testify to it. Forgiveness, compassion and solidarity will marks its members' dealings with one another and it will invest time in building a community life to express its core beliefs.

The calling of the Church to be a missionary community

If we go back to the day of Pentecost, the gift of the Spirit and the birth of the Church we notice that as well as reforming and renewing the Church community, the Spirit reignites mission. Driving the community out from their hide-away in the upper room they stand in the street and proclaim the truth about God in a multitude of languages. They offer the invitation to listeners to repent and discover the good news of Jesus and to be built into this kingdom community. Again this is a renewed, not a new, dimension to being in the gathered Jesus community. As a group they had been present and active with Jesus when he healed, when he fed large groups of hungry people, when he preached and taught in ways that opened people's eyes and hearts to God afresh, when he forgave sins and welcomed the marginalized. They had witnessed and been part of this mission as a band of disciples together. They had also been sent out in twos to do the same things – 'to proclaim the good news, . . . to cure the sick, raise the dead, cleanse the lepers, cast out demons' (Matthew 10.7–8) and they had seen the same divine reality breaking in through their shared missionary activities. What happened on the day of Pentecost was that this dimension to their calling was brought to life again, infused with the Holy Spirit.

The calling of the Church to act as a corporate missionary body is manifest throughout history. It can be traced through from the Acts of the Apostles and their commissioning of missionary pairs to spread the good news (Acts 13), its care for the poor of the ancient world, through its building of schools and hospitals, its campaigning for justice and reform of society, its action in humanitarian aid and above all for enterprising initiatives to proclaim the gospel and evangelize people far and wide even in the face of persecution. While in the history of the Church there are some remarkable individuals, who stand out for their passion and leadership in mission, in many more cases it is the Church acting as a body that has been effective.

Primitive Methodism is an interesting example in this regard. It is associated with key evangelistic figures such Hugh Bourne, William Clowes and Lorenzo Dow. By all accounts it was, in its early days, one of fastest expanding Christian movements in Britain, growing from zero to a quarter of a million members in less than 50 years and it was largely a church of the poor, drawing in and being led by labourers, miners and domestic servants more than any other nineteenth-century British church. While leadership was no doubt visionary and inspirational, you don't have to dig very deep to find that the real powerhouse of this missionary movement was ordinary people working together, acting as body. In Hugh Bourne's account of the first camp meeting[7] one senses that while the preaching was important in these outreach events, it was people praying

---

7 Hugh Bourne's account of the first camp meeting held on 31 May 1807. See *The History of the Methodist Church in Great Britain*, Vol. 4, London: Epworth 1988, pp. 316–21.

together that was the life source of the passion and energy. Here every-member ministry was seen in the love feasts, prayer meetings, classes and camp meetings that propelled mission. Naturally this same passion spilled over into the trade union movement, educational provision and political activism with Primitive Methodists providing leadership and energy for the reform and reshaping of society. It should not be surprising that this corporate body would produce men and women who would help others to act collectively to improve their lives.

Our own day is not lacking its witnesses to the calling of the Church to act as a missionary community. The will to do together those things that can embody and express God's love and transformative presence in the world can be seen in many places. Whether one looks at the phenomenon of the Alpha course, which one person has described as the 'busiest footpath to the front door of the Church over the past decade',[8] or at the initiatives of *Faithworks*[9] and the Church of England in taking over failing schools in deprived areas to seek to provide better education or at the campaign to stop sex trafficking, these are mission initiatives that rely on the church acting as a missionary community, using its organization and personnel to effect change.

Perhaps equally telling are the stories of small, often poorly resourced Christian communities acting together to take missionary action. Anne Morisy tells a story about one such church in Hackney responding to the needs of the homeless in the capital. Having agreed to participate in a scheme that involved several churches, this fearful but determined small group found ways of making a difference.

In order to keep open the doors of the church hall for just one evening and through the night, a whole network of helpers had to be lined up; far more than could be assembled from a worn-down congregation. The little team that took on the

---

8 Stuart Murray, *Church after Christendom*, Milton Keynes: Paternoster, 2004, p. 59.

9 See http://www.faithworks.info/

challenge in each of the participating churches had to recruit their friends and neighbours and neighbours' friends to do all that needed to be done.

Each evening the hall was open a team would be needed in the kitchen as well as welcoming people and clearing tables. Another team would take responsibility for getting the camp beds out helped by those who would be sleeping on them. There would also be a sleepover team and an early morning team to cook breakfast and clear everything away until the following week. But that is only half of it.

Behind the scenes were people such as those who would pop their newspaper through Betty's letterbox so she could take it with her to the hall for the homeless people to read. There were others who each week made meat balls and a large apple crumble in readiness for the supper that would be served to far more than those who slept overnight. Others washed and ironed the sheets and towels. The tired church halls might not look much but the bed linen was always freshly laundered.

The fact that so many people were desperate enough to bed down in a church hall in the back streets of Hackney came as a shock. The group who held the venture together had never expected such a high level of need. They found themselves more and more indignant that their basic and amateur provision was so urgently needed. That indignation translated into an invitation to the Member of Parliament to come to a meeting to discuss homelessness in Hackney.[10]

Much in recent writing has been about recovering of the calling of the Church community to shape its life and activity towards mission – to be a missionary community.

---

10 Ann Morisy, *Journeying Out*, London: Continuum, 2004, pp. 12–13.

A Church with three callings

So we have the calling of the Church in three directions:

- to be a kingdom community;
- to be a missionary community;
- to be a nurturing community that grows reflective disciples.

These are, of course, not separate, sealed parts of the Church's life but overlapping areas of what it means to be the Church.

Thus, when we begin to envision the Christian community, we cannot speak about building or shaping its life in relation to one of these alone. To do so is to court a distortion of our calling. The weakness of Haurerwas's view is that in putting so much weight on the life of the gathered Church he is in danger of denying the reality of God in the world, in the same way as some of the mission-shaped Church writers criticized in Chapter 3. At its extreme, this form of church is a sect, concerned entirely with its own inner life and uninterested in the wider world. It is a Disneyworld into which one escapes and its message to the world, if there is one, is come and join us for your world is not only corrupt but doomed and irredeemable.

Likewise, fixing our vision and directing our energy towards the Church as a missionary community exclusively may be to neglect both the quality of life that the kingdom represents and to ignore the presence of God throughout creation. At its extreme, this kind of Church is a form of global corporation seeking to reproduce its brand and products in the same form in every place. The missionary movements of the nineteenth century were prone to this neglect of context and blind to their own (often implicit) imperialism and the damage that such a single-minded focus for the Church produces.

A different kind of danger exists for those who build a Church with the single aim of supporting and nurturing disciples to be Christian travellers and traders in the world. The kind of Church outlined at the beginning of this chapter, were it to be pursued exclusively, could lose touch with the vision of the alternative society of the kingdom and neglect to act together in solidarity of mission with others. At its worst, it becomes a post-modern consumerist spirituality looking for glimpses of God with only a vague idea of the character of God revealed in Jesus and little notion of being a corporate body, let alone the body of Christ.

What we need is an integrated Church, one that recognizes the different dimensions of its calling and builds its life to sustain each. We must retain an emphasis on the daily needs of reflective disciples seeking the missionary God in the world and, at the same time, on the essential nature of the gathered community in its calling to be an alternative community and be collectively active in mission. That is why the notion of rhythm is so important. It is only by having a high view of the gathered Church and a high view of God's dispersed people in the world that we can create an expression of church that is faithful to the nature of God as Trinity and the *missio Dei*. As Ephesians 4 suggests, growth in the body of Christ and growth in the ways disciples live in the world mutually feed each other.[11]

Christian education

Our task therefore is to seek to build a Christian community that is true to its calling to be an alternative community, to be a missionary community and to be a community that supports and equips disciples to live faithful lives in the world. This building is a work of Christian education.

Christian education is not to be understood narrowly as courses, events and programmes that the Church designs and runs. Neither is it to be identified with the education offered to children and young people through church schools, RE lessons, Sunday schools, or youth groups. It is certainly not co-terminus with preaching and it is not only concerned with rational thinking and beliefs. It includes these, but Christian education is a much broader and more fundamental ministry. Christian education is concerned with helping people learn to live in a Christ-like way. This involves attitudes and actions,

---

11 See Chapter 4.

emotions and thoughts, experiences and lifestyle, individuals and communities all being fashioned after the pattern and person of Christ.[12]

Christian education is achieved through a variety of means, including relationships, the structures of the Church's life and many incidental and accidental dimensions of church life as well as its programmes and courses. Norma Everist records this well in the following paragraph:

> At small Grace Church community members continually teach and learn from one another. The couple who usher sometimes invite the children to join them in carrying the communion elements and basket from the food pantry to the altar. Young Cameron, living with muscular dystrophy, took his turn at ushering, maneuvering his wheel chair with the basket on his lap. A couple married for fifty years, by their presence, taught the young couple struggling to make it through five years of commitment. The organist, as she was battling cancer, taught the entire congregation how to die.[13]

Education by most definitions is intentional.[14] That is, it aims at producing learning, and therefore change, in learners. Some argue that it is also interventionist, that it is structured to intervene in the natural and intuitive processes of human life to achieve learning. As one person has said to me, 'Education is focused on those things which cannot be left to chance.' Both

---

12 Astley sets out a taxonomy of Christian education outcomes that includes attitudes and values, actions, experiences, beliefs (about and in) and emotions. See Jeff Astley, 'The Place of Understanding in Christianity and Education about Christianity', in Jeff Astley and Leslie Francis, *Critical Perspectives on Christian Education*, Leominster: Gracewing, 1992.

13 Norma Cook Everist, *The Church as Learning Community*, Nashville: Abingdon Press, 2002.

14 Commonly, teaching is defined as 'action undertaken with the intention to bring about learning', and education as 'the planned, purposeful provision of learning opportunities, as for example, in a national system of education, or a school curriculum'.

these ideas need some refinement in the light of the examples given above. In the case of the organist, the intention was to seek to live in the face of pain and death in a way that reflected faith in Christ. This was not in the first instance an intention to bring about learning in others but in a Christian community setting that is exactly what happened. We might say it became educational because the learners in that church community were also seeking how to be more Christ-like and the intention of the learners encountered an authentic example of what they were seeking. And this can only happen because the Christian community is essentially structured for such learning. This should be no surprise to us, for we noted above that Jesus drew people into a relationship with him and others precisely so that learning could happen. People networked together in relationship with Jesus will affect each other as they are affected by him. Likewise, it is interventionist not in the sense that someone has constructed a programme to draw people out of their normal lives and patterns but in the foundational sense that God has intervened in history and called into being a new community to live in a different way. In this alternative society education is part of the ground plan of the Church. Stanley Hauerwas once wrote: 'The church does not "do" religious education . . . The church is a form of education.'[15] Because it is a group of people in relationship with God through Christ, because it tells a story about how the world is, based on the life, death and resurrection of Jesus, because it is engaged in living together as a radical new and alternative community, it has a built-in pedagogical dynamic. Its goals are to respond to God's love, and to help others to be part of the transformative work that God is doing in the world. In other words, it seeks Christ-likeness in itself and in others, and its structure, proclamation and activities are geared towards change, formation and transformation. Christian education is in this sense another way of talking about being church.

---

15 Stanley Hauerwas, 'The Gesture of a Truthful Story', in Jeff Astley et al., *Theological Perspectives on Christian Formation*, p. 97.

This is not an excuse for not planning or running programmes or courses such as *Emmaus* or forming cell groups or organizing a Bible study. It is important, however, to make this broader claim about Christian education before turning to specific suggestions and ideas or we may miss the most critical aspect of Christian education. Before any Alpha course is put on, before any small group is formed, or Lent programme devised, Christian education is operating in a church, either attracting, forming and transforming people or leaving them untouched, unengaged or even driven away. In its practice of gathering together for worship and ordering its life, in its people and their relationships with each other, in its simple routines for sharing bread and wine, welcoming newcomers or using its financial resources, in the quality of spirituality and its expressions of compassion, forgiveness and delight, it offers a potent learning environment.

The courses and events that we put on should be done to meet specific needs identified in the church's life within this wider framework of Christian education, not as a substitute for it. Ignoring the implicit educational dynamic of the Church is dangerous and can be counter productive. Many churches have run Alpha courses, for example, with little or no 'success'. Despite its demonstrable success in a variety of contexts, it has not worked for them. There are always many different possible reasons for something not working, but for some churches the course has been undermined by the church's normal life and worship, which did not match up to the Alpha experience. Where a course resonates with the church's ethos and convictions it is far more likely to be effective. Interestingly, where churches have adopted forms of Alpha that fit better with their core spirituality and churchmanship, or developed their own enquirers' course they have been more successful in terms of people making a commitment of faith.[16]

We should expect to run events and programmes on a regular basis but we should also expect to attend to the Christian

---

16 Mike Booker and Mark Ireland, *Evangelism – which way now?*, London: Church House Publishing, 2003, p. 35.

education implicit in the life of the church. To use a different kind of metaphor, a garden already planted has a shape and seasonal cycle of its own. It needs to be attended to on a regular basis to maintain this and to allow it to be in best condition and shape. One can add new plants, shrubs, bushes and trees, indeed any enthusiastic or serious gardener will want to do so, but she or he needs to work with the aesthetic and organic dynamics of the garden to develop it well. If you choose to plant a leylandii tree in the middle of your rose bed, it may not only look odd but may damage the roses too.

So, Christian education is about attending to the implicit learning dynamic of the Church community *and* addressing specific needs through the provision of training and educational activities. In what follows we will outline ways of seeing and approaching Christian education in relation to the three callings of the Church. Doing Christian education well is building the Church to be effective in each different sphere.

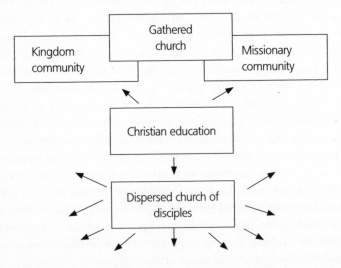

In relation to each sphere we will identify where the key dialogue lies, what approaches are likely to be resonant with the aspect of church we are seeking to grow and indicate briefly some useful programmes.

Christian education for a kingdom community

Dialogue

The core dialogue for Christian education to attend to in building a kingdom community is the conversation between the vision of the kingdom and the lived life of the gathered community. In simplistic terms this is asking how our living together matches or fails to match the Sermon on the Mount or early Christian community as recorded in Acts. I use the word simplistic because this conversation cannot only be a direct one. As I argued in Chapter 4, being faithful may not mean doing the same things, but undertaking new things that honour the reality behind those original expressions. There are in history and in other parts of the world Church, different patterns that may help us to see what to live as a kingdom community is like. Nevertheless, the core discipline is careful attention to the life and teaching of Jesus and critical reflection on how we are to embody that now.

Approaches

1 Foundations

In order for any building and shaping of the kingdom community to happen, some basic elements need to be in place. The kingdom is unlikely to grow where there is no desire for it, no love of the gospel story, no willingness to accept its claims upon our lives, no mutuality or even willingness to listen to others, no place for conversation and reflection and no openness to change and growth. This is very stony ground, but sadly some communities that go by the name of church meet most of these hallmarks. For such communities, which have completely lost sight of the kingdom, or perhaps for those beginning from scratch in planting a new form of church, these will be core qualities to nurture. Steven Croft has argued that the renewal of the Church in these times of transition will come through the formation of small groups where such passions and attitudes can be nurtured and grow:

It is my contention that the malaise of the church in main-stream denominations is due at least in part to the neglect of that aspect of church life which can be expressed in these small groups: depth of friendship, and relationship; disciple-ship within a structure of mutual accountability; worship and prayer which arise from and are closely related to shared lives; the common sense of purpose enabling one another to share the mission of God.[17]

Establishing a single small group that rekindles a fire for the kingdom and builds together the beginnings of a living king-dom community will be perhaps the single most important Christian education action that can be taken. Such a group may have to step back from major mission initiatives, or rather let them grow more gradually out of their reformed life. It may also have to take to itself the burden of supporting members in their dispersed discipleship, though in a small group this can often be integrated very naturally with the desire to be a king-dom community. It may be that such a group could be helped by adopting or developing for itself a simple rule of life, not unlike the covenant discipleship model outlined below. This way of prayer, study, action and accountability may be at the heart of the meetings and provides a structured way of praying for and supporting each other.

Croft calls these small groups 'transforming communities' and likens their role to that of trellis on which a vine may grow. The trellis does not determine the particular form and shape of the vine but supplies for it anchor points that allow the vine freedom to flourish and develop.

2 Focus on events

Let us assume now that some of the foundations are in place. It is not that we have no sense or love of the kingdom but we wish to nurture, tend and develop its reality in our midst. One approach to this is what Charles Forster calls 'events centred

---

17 Steven Croft, *Transforming Communities*, London: Darton, Long-man & Todd, 2002, p. 72.

education'.[18] This is where events in the life of the Church intentionally become the focus for the gathered community to reflect and deepen their sense of who they are called to be. The events may be *seasonal events* – events connected with the liturgical calendar plus local events; *occasional events* – weddings, funerals, missions, weekends away; *paradigmatic events* – key events in the history of a denomination, ethnic group or local church; or *unexpected events* – such as a sudden community tragedy or the hosting of some major event in the locality. Because any of these will naturally be a focus, it is relatively easy to develop them into a special focus and people may be able to give time for more in-depth work and reflection. Forster suggests in order to make these events meaningful learning occasions there need to be: **Preparation** which will include familiarization with stories, texts, roles, action and so on (with enough practice so that participants feel unselfconscious); **engagement** so that the acting or reading or creative art or music involves people physically and mentally; and **critical reflection** in planned (as well as unplanned) conversations, so as to encourage sharing the meanings we draw from it.

One church where I was minister for a time produced several Roger Jones musicals for Easter, Pentecost and Christmas. Each provided an all-age event and a variety of ways of involving almost everyone in the small Christian community. 'Doing the show' was always satisfying, especially as, despite lots of practice, it always looked as if we would not be ready, the day before. This was in part because as we prepared various elements – singing, acting, costumes and props or dance – we had conversations about what we were doing and why and whether this was the right way to interpret the story. We might find ourselves getting out Bibles and reading passages, and inevitably someone saying 'Do you think it means this, and if so, what should we do in our church?' Occasionally, we disagreed with the words or sentiments in the production and changed it. Some of the house groups discussed the different accounts

18 Charles R. Foster, *Educating Congregations,* Nashville: Abingdon Press, 1994.

in the Gospels and where they differed and sometimes the portrayals cut deep and a person who had played the part of a forgiven man or women connected this with something in their own life and felt real healing or the need to ask for someone's forgiveness.

The musicals were always fine on the day, of course, like so many other theatre-type productions, but over and above this, the growth in Christian community was tangible for the participants. Events education of this kind can be very effective because the learning about Christian community is resonant with the medium. People learn from each other about Christian community in a church community activity that is informed by the vision and reality of Christian community in the scriptures.

3 Attention to practices

Within the field of social learning theory much has been made of what are called communities of practice. These are social communities characterized by a series of regular, routine or ritualized activities, which may be called practices. It is easy to see that church would fit this description. Gathered church communities offer worship to God, say prayers, read the scriptures and seek to interpret these, have rituals for welcoming new members (baptism), affirming their full participation (confirmation), and marking moments in the life journey (weddings and funerals); most share bread and wine in a ritualized way, they organize social events, run kids' clubs, have structured ways for confessing faults and failings and give money to the church and charitable causes. For most members it is the doing of these things that constitutes the heart of their involvement. People may say it is the meaning behind all these that matters but their time is largely given to this doing.

According to this particular view, meaning is not a separate thing from doing but is deeply tied in with action. For it is through regular participation in the practices of a community that people negotiate meaning and come to know it for themselves. This does not mean that they have an abstract knowledge in the dictionary or encyclopedia sense. Rather, they know in a meaningful way as they participate.

I remember Mary, a Methodist communion steward telling me about how she undertook her responsibility and what it meant. Her job was to set out the table once a month for communion, which meant washing the cloths and making sure they were pristine white, filling the chalice and little cups in the trays with wine, and preparing the bread. During communion she would invite groups forward to take the elements and make sure that everyone, including the infirm, was able to share and then, when all had been served, she would go forward and receive communion with the last rail of folk. Afterwards she would wash up and clear things away, feed any leftover bread to the birds and take home the cloths for washing. 'I feel so close to God', she said, 'as I get things ready. It is as if I am getting a meal table ready for God to come to. I make sure it is the very best I can make it so that it looks good when the cloth is lifted from over the elements. I feel that something marvellous is happening when people go forward and kneel and receive. Then at the end I also am able to share these gifts from God. There is such a joy in my heart that often I find myself singing when I am washing up and feeding the birds. I don't mind being late home on those days because I feel I am loved and trusted by God.'

Mary may not have a fully developed theology of holy communion – though I suspect she could articulate its meaning better than many – but she did have an understanding of what was happening when she was participating in this regular church practice. She had negotiated meaning for herself and she knew it most intensely at the point of participation. What she told me was, of course, a secondary reflection, an abstraction, a narrative to express what she knew at a deeper, more profound, level when it was happening. Some parts of knowledge are extractable and can be expressed in words but some parts are tacit, they are within people and are only encountered and experienced when they are acted out.

Practices are themselves complex and full of intended meaning. They have been created, developed and continue to evolve to carry meaning within the community. The pattern of communion in which Mary participated was, of course, not her invention and neither was her interpretation of what she was doing built out of nothing. She had heard lots of sermons about holy communion, she had experienced the liturgical words many hundreds of times, she had observed its setting with the architecture of the building, from Mavis and Harry, communion stewards before her, she had learned how to get the table ready, and she may have talked about communion at her house group. She would only be vaguely aware of most of these things but, in effect, through them she was drawing on the Church's accumulated meaning, located in the artefact, stories, images and conceptualizations of the community.

Christian education for a kingdom community can gain much from attention to practices. Conversation between people about what they do and what it means will open up a variety of interpretations and perspectives where people will help each other and may even challenge views. There are, of course, no right answers in such sharing but it can be a gateway to exploring other interpretations from the tradition and entering into a dialogue, the fashioning of a new meaning, and perhaps even changes in practice.

4 Audits and visitations

The perspective of newcomers is a vital one but soon lost. Newcomers see with fresh eyes what is going on and they spot the mismatch between what we say and what we do, which we no longer notice. The longer they are with a community, however, the more likely it is that they will have become embedded in the shared patterns and self-understandings that the community holds, and can no longer hold a mirror up for us. We need to harness the clear-sightedness while it is fresh. Some denominations have arrangements or programmes for visitation or review. That is, a person, perhaps in office such as an archdeacon, or a group from another church or circuit will spend some time with a church community and feed back what they see. This should be in the form of an affirmation of things that stand out as positively conveying the Christian message, and constructive criticism in identifying the weaknesses of our shared life and mission. They may even be able to recommend an action or programme or initiative that may strengthen our life. Like sensitive and loving truth-speaking for individuals, this process can be challenging and renewing. If this does not exist for your church network, ask someone or a group to help you review your Christian community. There are some self-audits too[19] which are useful, though these lack the sharp outsider view.

5   Education for worship

In my experience, one of the most effective forms of deepening understanding about what it means to be a kingdom community is when people are involved in preparing and leading worship. In this place whether as a preacher, worship leader, member of team or occasional contributor, people have to come to a view about what it is we are trying to say or celebrate, have to try to communicate this and may need to negotiate this meaning with others in the process, especially if part of a team. The young dance group at the church in Liverpool where I was minister negotiated meaning about their faith on a weekly basis – I suspect more than in the confirmation classes they attended – with each other and the other leaders of worship. They read the readings for the Sunday and talked about music, words and themes in the service before trying out moves and sequences and then constructively commenting on what they were doing to make it better. 'I am not sure those movements convey what we mean by Christian hope', one might say. Others might agree or put a different point of view and then they would try another way of approaching the dance. By the Sunday, the performed dance

---

19 The Methodist Church offers a pack entitled *Pilgrims Way* for Circuit and Church reviews, which can be undertaken with help from a partner outside the local setting. The Baptist Union provides a Mission Consultancy programme and the United Reformed Church is developing a Mission and Ministry Review.

was very often moving and evocative but even when it was neither you could be sure that they knew a great deal more about the theme of the day because they had wrestled with it to create the dance.

There are, of course, formal training programmes for preachers and worship leaders. These are to be used and many of them are open to others who may not sense a calling to this ministry but who would gain greatly from participating. But the growing multi-voice and multi-media approaches to worship allow even more people to be actors in the creating and leading of worship, and provide opportunities to run local short courses and develop a reflective team approach to worship preparation.

Christian education for a missionary community

Dialogue

The conversation at the heart of this calling is the dialogue between faith and culture, between church and wider society. It is concerned with what visible forms expressing God's mission should take for a gathered community and will draw heavily on careful investigative analysis of what is happening in the context of the Christian community. This has often been connected with a locality – how should the church act in a public way to respond to the needs of their immediate area, village or town? – but in new forms of church there may be different expressions. For example, a community with a number of suitably experienced teachers and worship leaders might create a website offering free, high-quality resources for school assemblies that meets a regional or national need. Educationally, the task here is to translate the mission of God to heal, to restore, to include, to forgive, to bring justice, friendship and reconciliation into forms that can communicate with the people of our time.

Approaches

1   Getting started: learning the language of mission

As with so many other aspects of Christian education people often learn by doing. About six years ago North Road Methodist Church, Durham decide to start a Friday luncheon club. It was an easy thing for this community to do. It had premises close to the heart of the city and right next to the bus station. There were several members who were skilled at catering, some with professional backgrounds, and there were sufficient retired people with time to give and a few students who could usually find a couple of hours on a Friday to help. It was to be called MANNAS (after the Old Testament 'manna' feeding God's people on the move). As it was conceived, the talk was about providing good food, a sense of community and an informal listening service, in that one person was always free to roam tables and settle in for a chat with folk on their own or those who seemed troubled. The good humour of the volunteers and the quality of the food soon attracted a regular clientele of 70–100 people over the couple of hours it was open each Friday. Some found their way to the worshipping community but this was not particularly sought or promoted. What was significant, however, was that through this initiative the congregation began to own the language of mission. They were doing something together to connect with the community that was growing out of their understanding of God and it soon translated into other activities: opening their church overnight for prayer with imaginative prayer stations – on a Friday night on a street with many pubs and clubs; offering a Christmas day fun lunch for those on their own (singles or couples), which brought together, among others, students from overseas and people from the mental health club; and starting a conversation with other churches about providing street pastors. Meanwhile, its worshipping congregation grew.

This is not a traditional evangelical church but it is a growing, lively missionary community whose worship as well as its lunch club is infused with energy. By taking some action to connect with the people of its natural sphere of life, the Christians of this church began to reflect on what mission means and found that it grew and developed.

The key to mission education is doing and reflecting.

2 Action and reflection

Without conversation both beforehand and as it happened, the North Road lunch club would not have become the missional launch pad that it evolved to be. The scheme needed to be in touch with the gospel in such a way that a mutual critique could occur. What I mean is that those running the club and the wider church community needed to be asking how this was expressing God's love in Christ and where they were being led. They needed to shape the club to be a visible expression of what they believed about God and to look at the concrete reality of the Friday luncheon club to help them see more clearly what the gospel might mean in a tangible form. This helped them to understand the gospel better and to assess how they were doing at the same time. Had this not occurred, the club could have been simply a good eating place with cheap food and satisfied clients, giving a buzz to the volunteers, popular and located as part of the consumerist culture – nothing wrong with that in itself but not necessarily mission.

Ann Morisy has some important things to say about projects that become separated from the church community and are driven by a society agenda that only emphasizes needs-meeting.

When a church or project gets caught up in a needs-meeting perspective it puts the Church and the congregation in a position of superiority. Those 'out there' are the ones in need, whilst those within the Church have the capacity to help. This may be a caricature, but nevertheless needs-meeting as an aim must imply that those who are needy are in some way in deficit, whilst competence and resourcefulness are retained in the hands of the helper. The Gospel with its capacity to overturn everyday assumptions will have none of this. The gracious processes that Jesus demonstrates make it clear that it is the needy who carry the transformational potential. The radical actions of Jesus up-end the taken-for-granted pattern of giving and receiving. Furthermore, unless we can free ourselves from the liberal mantra of needs-meeting, we may miss the real blessings and gracefulness associated with journeying out – without the expectation being able to meet people's needs.[20]

In order to keep close to the good news we need to reflect on our actions.

Action–reflection is an interactive process. It is really action–reflection–action–reflection–action . . . recurring. There should be no time when seeking to relate our corporate actions to the gospel becomes unnecessary or superfluous. It should be built into the daily life of the church as we negotiate meaning in these practices but it should also be considered from time to time with some time and theological resource to guide and refine our action. One church in the heart of London holds an annual theological reflection day on its vast social and mission programme with a view to understanding more fully what it is doing and why and considering whether some things should be brought to an end and other things begun.

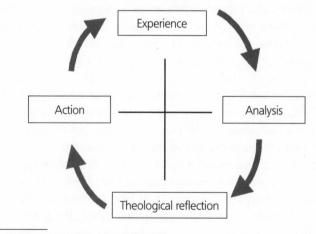

20 Morisy, *Journeying Out*, p. 27.

A slightly more sophisticated form of this action–reflection model is found in the pastoral cycle.

This particular model is very useful as a 'learning for action and learning from action' approach to mission. It helps to answer the question 'How should we do this better?' but builds in another more important question, namely, 'How does what we do fit with our belief about God's character and work in the world and our calling to be the Church sharing in God's mission?'

Beginning with some experience or issue, or our current practice (*experience*) the group builds up a picture of what is going on by gathering information and perhaps looking at the experience through different lenses with the help of, for example, sociology, psychology or economics (*analysis*). Then through identifying particular faith questions raised and seeking what the Bible and Christians have said in the past and present, theological reflection takes place (*theological reflection*). At this point the group seeks a coherence of belief about God and action that can be owned by the community. Then action is planned and taken (*action*), which of course leads to new experience and the cycle begins again.

An example of this is a church being offered a large cheque for some of its land by a development company eager to build a new shopping complex (*experience*). At first sight this is a boon to the congregation who are struggling to maintain its extensive premises. On further analysis, the church sees that the changing pattern of shopping in the town will make it harder for those who are least mobile and least wealthy while meeting the needs of many of the more wealthy in the town and the new shopping centre will simply add to this divide (*analysis*). Later when it is considered at the PCC, someone is asked to present a short talk on stewardship and the use of land in the Bible. Here people notice that much is said in the Old Testament about making provision for the poor in the use of the land (see, for example, Exodus 23.11; Leviticus 19.10; Deuteronomy 15) and, as a result, the church asks to talk to the developer about a variety of issues to enable the less wealthy to be included (*theological reflection* leading to proposed *action*). One result is the provision of a shop space at a peppercorn rent for a charity shop that will make clothes and other goods available to the least wealthy.[21]

Whatever ways are used, some theological reflection on our missionary action is necessary for learning and development.

3 Making disciples

One of the most pressing needs for all churches is to make new disciples. This is not a 'bums on seats' project to save the faltering church, it is rather of the essence of the missional calling of the Church. Jesus' last command, according to Matthew, is to 'Go therefore and make disciples of all nations, baptizing them in the name of the Father and of the Son and of the Holy Spirit, and teaching them to obey everything that I have commanded you' (Matthew 28.19–20).

Here there has been great activity in the last 15 years. *Alpha* boasts that over 2 million people in Britain and over 13 million worldwide have attended Alpha courses.[22] This has given rise to dozens of Alpha-look-alike programmes or at least courses that have adopted its template of meals, input group discussion and weekends away in order to invite individuals to consider Christian faith.

The Christian education issue is how to go about this in a way that tackles the task with integrity as well as effectiveness. Going for a quick fix, ready-made programme is attractive but should be cautiously avoided. We have already mentioned the problems of a course that does not resonate with the church community that uses it. Not only is it usually ineffective but can also make for dispirited people and undermine confidence for other ventures. It may also reveal a misguided focus on

---

21 D. Durston, 'Theological reflection – Historical Faith in Dialogue with Contemporary Experience', in the *British Journal of Theological Education*, Vol. 3 no. 3, Summer 1990, pp. 36–47. See also Paul H. Ballard and J. Pritchard, *Practical Theology in Action*, London: SPCK, 1996.

22 Alpha website (http://uk.alpha.org) April 2009.

getting numbers in rather than on making disciples. Making disciples is more than getting people to a first commitment or experience of God. In post-modern culture seeking experiences is a common desire but translating that into long-term committed discipleship may require more thought.

Empirical evidence and theological conviction suggests the following approach.

1 Make your own

Devise and run a course that the church community can own. All the evidence is that those who do are effective. While Alpha created a template of effective ingredients – sharing a meal, simple presentation, a no holds barred small group discussion, a timely weekend away and a genuine willingness to let people decide for themselves – the content and ethos needs to echo the spirituality of the Christian community that runs the programme. Look at the range available. Pilot more than one course with committed members. This will not only help you to see what fits well with the ethos of the church but also gives potential leaders a real experience of doing the course. Adapt and modify and if you feel you are straying too far from the original or there is pressure to conform 'for quality assurance purposes' set to and write your own.

2 Have a long-term view

The evidence of both people leaving the church and people joining is that it takes two to three years for the process to happen.[23] Programmes that run for six weeks or twelve weeks need to be part of a longer process. Martyn Atkins has made a good argument for restoring a new form of the catechumenate[24] – the pattern of preparation for joining the Church that operated in the early centuries of the Christian era. This clearly needs to be re-invented for the twenty-first century but much work

---

23 Philip Richter and Leslie Francis, *Gone but Not Forgotten*, London: Darton, Longman & Todd, 1998.

24 Martyn Atkins, *Resourcing Renewal: Shaping Churches for the Emerging Future*, Peterborough: Inspire, 2007, pp. 174ff.

has already been done within the Roman Catholic and Anglican churches on this front.[25] One of the additional strengths of the catechetical pattern is its emphasis on learning to practise habits, attitudes and sensibilities and the use of mentors as well as programmes of instruction. Whatever the pattern, helping people move from an enquirer stage to long-term discipleship is likely to be more effective if nurtured over a period of two years or more.

3 Embed it in the regular life of the church

Churches that have tried Alpha once or twice and given up on it, or keep in mind to run it again as and when needed, have tended to be less effective than those who have embedded it in their ongoing life – one or twice or more every year. The mistake seems to be to try it to see if it works, whereas the aim should be to establish a pattern that nurtures disciples as a core part of the life of the church.[26]

4 Aim to make reflective disciples

Build a course that from the beginning aims to make reflective disciples. That is, disciples who will take up the challenge to be sent into the world to meet with God, to shape the world and be shaped themselves throughout life, to travel and trade, to translate between the dispersed and gathered communities and to grow in and through courageous openness, accountability, immersion in the tradition and constant prayerfulness – in other words, people who live in the rhythm. These outcomes are not add-ons, or extras for those who succeed in the knock-out stages. These characteristics are what all disciples are called to

---

25 Liam Kelly, *Catechesis Revisited*, London: Darton, Longman & Todd, 2000. M. Jane Carew (ed.), *Making Disciples: A Comprehensive Catechesis for the RCIA*, Our Sunday Visitor Inc., US, 1997. Peter Ball and Malcolm Grundy, *Faith on the Way: A Practical Parish Guide to the Adult Catechumenate*, London: Mowbray, 2000.

26 Charles Freebury, *Assessing Today's Top Evangelistic Courses* (September 2004) – available as download from the Emmaus website (http://www.e-mmaus.org.uk/emm_section.asp?id=2380897).

and people should get some sense of these at the very outset of the programme. Good educational designers have the intended outcomes in mind before they devise the course. It is exactly this outcome orientation that can help create the structure and choose the appropriate methods. If you have people who will attend church in mind as an outcome then that is probably what you will get. Our aim, however, is to make disciples.

Christian education for nurturing disciples

Dialogue

Most of this book has been concerned with the dialogue between the experience of God in the gathered community and that of individual disciples in their daily lives. This dialogue assumes that God the Trinity who creates community is also the missionary God who is active in the world and meets, speaks to and shapes life and people in the world as well as in the gathered Church. The burden of our theme has been the neglect of this aspect of our calling and the structuring or the re-structuring of the Church to address the needs of disciples dispersed into the life of the world to 'work out their salvation in fear and trembling' (Philippians 2.12).

All the dialogues that we have identified in which Christian education needs to operate are difficult – most genuine two-way conversations make demands – but this particular dialogue presents us with even more challenges. For here disciples encounter a world in which there are many issues not previously encountered, more questions than answers and many of the pre-formed answers that the Church has built up over centuries and through several shifts of culture either do not fit or cause serious dissonance. We have hinted at some of these already, especially in Chapter 2. Christian education is particularly difficult here, for the gathered Church finds it much easier to proclaim, direct and give answers than it does to hear, reflect and change – especially in the belief zone. Hence all the approaches suggested depend also on the Church finding new forms of listening and re-forming, or living with unresolved diversity, confident that God holds all things together.

Approaches

1 First steps

Some gathered church communities have no idea what members do with the majority of their time. Simple first steps are to find out from each other and to create ways of praying for each other. This can be achieved by an internal audit, asking people to say or write something about what occupies most of their time, where that is and what they do. One can also ask about voluntary involvements and families. If you are bold you can ask people to make one prayer request. This can be done in small groups, if the church is large. Another possibility is to establish a prayer rota or prayer card in which certain groups, occupations or areas of life of the congregation are regularly prayed for. Start a reflection of the month (or week) in which someone talks about how their faith impacts on some part of their life. If you don't have it already, introduce a regular 'where I have seen God at work' conversation slot into worship or small group gatherings.

To sustain a deeper level of reflective discipleship more is needed.

2 Connections programmes

The core discipline for reflective disciples is to engage regularly in making connections. We noted in the 'treasuring and pondering' (Luke 2.19) process that although some of the deep transformative connections and insights cannot be rushed, nevertheless the practice of making connections is a vital skill to nurture. One of the ways this is beginning to emerge in my own church denomination is the development of vocational learning and reflection. This at the moment goes by the initials EDEV, which stands for Extending Discipleship, Exploring Vocation. It aims to allow people at particular points in their life to take some time to ask 'What does God want me to do?' The structure of the programme is deliberately loose but offers people four ways to explore this question: by sharing with others in groups their story, their gifts, their passion and personalities; by studying more about some aspect of the faith; by extending their experience to accompany another person in their vocation and reflect on the placement; and by investigating more deeply their own church tradition. The elements continually open the question in a different way. The outcome may be that people find some other vocational direction, or take a small step in assuming a new responsibility in the gathered church but many, perhaps most who have participated in the early pilots of the programme have felt that this has enabled them to do what they were doing already – in everyday work, family and community – but with a stronger sense of connectedness with their faith.

In Hertfordshire for a time I worked with another person developing work–theology groups. We invited people to attend a series of six to ten sessions where the main topic of conversation would be their work. The two facilitators, myself and another minister, simply asked each in turn to tell the group about their work, skills, pressures, dilemmas and frustrations. Those attending the groups were consistently surprised that the first couple of meetings were given solely to this so that everyone in the group had a sense of what the others did. Then at the end of the second meeting we posed a question to come to answer the next week such as 'In your place of work where is there creativity?' or 'Where is pain experienced in your work life and who experiences it most acutely?' Each week they came and made their contributions to the questions and then we asked them to say how this connected to their faith. By session five the group would be buzzing with theological conversation and folk could not wait to attend. At the end of the programme, one person said, 'I never thought God was in that place' (their place of work), an interesting echo of Genesis 28.16.

Art and creative activities can also provide the opportunity to make connections but with less immediate emphasis on the words and discussion. Groups that paint and pray together, or have reflection sessions that involve working with clay or crea-tive writing or photography, or explore Christian (and other forms of) art can find stimulating ways of making connections and linking different parts of their lives at levels other than simply the rational reasoned meaning-making that often char-acterizes house or home groups.

3 Covenanted groups

Covenant discipleship groups have been established in North America for about 30 years now. They were the brain child of David Lowes Watson growing out of his research work on the early Methodist class system and his desire to find a form of small groups to fulfil the same functions of accountability, prayer and support. At core, a covenant discipleship group is a small number of people (usually seven) who commit them-selves to meet regularly and hold each other to account for how they live out their Christian faith. Using four key elements of discipleship (compassion, justice, devotion and worship) the members together draw up a covenant and meet to check with each other how they are getting on in their commitment.[27] The weekly group meeting lasts only one hour and remains focused on accountability, with members sharing their experience and supporting, praying for and encouraging one another in their discipleship. After the opening prayers, the leader encourages the group to read out the text they have composed together and then asks each person to give an account, working through the clauses of the covenant. This may include personal clauses, for which an individual has asked the group to hold him/her accountable. This regular focused accounting offers a way of striving for more faithful discipleship in a context of support and prayerful encouragement.

---

27 For a fuller description see 'Covenant Discipleship: The New Class Meeting?', *Epworth Review*, Vol. 33 No. 2, April 2006, pp. 54–63. David Lowes Watson, *Covenant Discipleship: Christian Forma-tion through Mutual Accountability*, Nashville: Discipleship Resources, 1991.

The wording and content of the covenant is in the hands of the group, which means that it can be related to the situations and commitments of the particular group of disciples, though the template is provided so as to ensure that members look outward as well as inward, to the public sphere as well as to the private. Thus, while acts of compassion may be at an individual level, a commitment to justice often involves people being active in their community, workplace or national life in issues of integrity, fairness and truth. These justice issues are, however, identified by the individuals and thus each person seeks to discover how she or he is being called to live as a disciple in his or her life. In this way the covenant, while remaining firmly located within a broad concept of Christian discipleship, is made concrete and applied to particular settings.

This programme has had some considerable success in the US but has been slow to translate into the UK context. At the moment, only a handful of groups exist here but the approach, if it can be adapted to the British context, promises much. One way the Methodist Church may develop this is through combining the covenant disciples approach with the current membership ticket, which identifies the four areas of discipleship outlined in the *Our Calling* statement, adopted by the Methodist Church in 2000.

Even if it does not catch on in this form, the movement towards accountability groups is growing. Cell groups work in this way and there is evidence that they are increasingly moving towards covenant-based patterns to support disciples in their daily lives. New monasticism, as it called, also offers this kind of approach, often focusing the dispersed communities on a shared rule of life which the community develops together.

Such covenanted approaches have the strength of being able to hold together different ways of a dispersed life and providing a meeting point for faith to relate to all parts. They may also provide a place to tell stories from individual lives and offer experiences or dilemmas for group discussion.

Conclusion: Educating the reflective disciple[28]

What has been offered here by way of Christian education for each of the three callings is only indicative and suggestive. Much more is available by way of resources and infinitely more by way of possibility. The hope has been to allow you to consider the three callings and check out your own church's provision. It is almost certainly the case that Christian education for one of the three will be more developed than the others. Perhaps this will stimulate you to see what you could do in relation to another dimension of the Church's calling. My guess is that, for many, the neglected one will be the support and learning offered to nurture disciples in their calling to transform the world and my hope is that by focusing most of the book on the importance of discipleship lived in the midst of the messy, muddled, post-modern world, you may be inspired to revisit this as a key priority in your life and church. Writing the book has confronted me again with the need to discover and affirm the call of discipleship and nurture in myself and others the capacity to be faithful reflective disciples.

28 This phrase is a deliberate echoing of the title of one of Donald Schön's books: Donald A. Schön, *Educating the Reflective Practitioner: Toward a New Design for Teaching and Learning in the Professions*, The Jossey-Bass Higher Education Series, San Francisco: Jossey-Bass, 1987.